Which Cat

Compiled and edited by Robert Duffy

An essential guide to the UK's most popular cats

Perfect-Pets

636.608

JO

Renfrewshire
Council

MAY 2021

The library is always open at
renfrewshirelibraries.co.uk

Visit now for library news and
information,
to renew and
reserve online, and
to download
free eBooks.

LISA
JACKS

Phone: 0300 300 1188
Email: libraries@renfrewshire.gov.uk

Published in Great Britain in 2020 by
BX Plans Ltd.
Remus House
Coltsfoot Drive
Peterborough
PE2 9BF
Telephone 01733 898103
www.perfect-pets.org

SB ISBN 978-1-91329-619-3
Photographs: Adobe Stock

Contents

Introduction

People tend to think that the world is divided into people who have cats and those who don't. This type of mentality is especially so among dog owners, many of whom say they would never dream of "crossing over" into the cat world. Of course, many animal lovers keep both cats and dogs, and always have, so this type of divided loyalty is artificial, and probably very 21st century.

The fact is that cats make superb pets, and you can guarantee that any cat you keep under your roof will have its own personality. It may be true that cats are less "useful" than some dogs in some ways; but for many families and individuals, having a non-human friend with a real character is very rewarding. You may not be able to take it for walks or teach it tricks, but a cat has its own way of letting you know it loves you.

Cats are defamed among dog lovers for being disloyal; that they will go to any household which is prepared to feed them, and show no gratitude afterwards. As we will see in this guide, this is simply not true; cats are very territorial, and your home - and those who live in it - will be at the centre of that territory. Cats may be able to better look after themselves than dogs, but they know very well the true value of home.

One thing that is generally true when comparing cats to dogs is that cats are relatively much cheaper to keep than dogs. They look after their own exercise, and are happy to eat exactly what you give them, at the same times every day. As most dogs will require a lot of attention and exercise, this makes cats a good choice for busy people.

So, if you're thinking of venturing into the world of cats, read on. Here we present the top 25 breeds of feline friend in the world at the moment, with each of their pros and cons. You're doing the right thing by carrying out research first, so we hope this will help you take the next step and enjoy the company of a cat for life.

Life Span

Of the many things which separate cats and dogs, life span is one of the most obvious. A domestic cat can live up to 20 years, which is extremely rare for any type of dog. Actual lifespan will depend on a number of factors, of course, but there is every chance the kitten to buy or adopt today could still be with you in two decades' time.

One of the reasons for this long life expectancy is the fact that cats' lives have six distinct stages (not the nine lives of popular myth). Each of these sees your cat develop certain facets which are really quite noticeable among experienced cat owners. With the right timing and interventions, the graduation from one stage to the next can be managed to make it as smooth as possible, giving your cat a happy, healthy life as you help it progress through its natural life cycle.

Here are the stages:

1 Kitten (0 - 6 months)

This is by far the best time to take a cat on, as you can influence its future life in a number of vital ways. Kittens experience the biggest growth spurt of any cat's life cycle, and need to be socialized during this time. You should introduce your kitten to other pets if you have them, and pet them yourself to get them used to human contact. Introducing them to children at this stage is also essential, and it is a good idea to have a kitten neutered now. It is a fact that neutered cats live longer, and an unneutered cat will very soon produce litters of its own, either as a father or mother.

2 Junior (6 months - 2 years)

Cats reach sexual maturity at about 6 months, which is why you should have yours neutered beforehand, unless you intend to breed, and are fully prepared for this. Still a surprisingly young age, your junior cat will also learn behaviours which will stay with them for life. You should play with them, but not roughly; if they expect a fight every time they see people, they will prepare for one. Use cat toys, which are specially designed to engage their natural curiosity. Also, teach your children not to be rough with junior; as their claws soon become long and sharp, as do their teeth. Remember, all cats are related; from the cutest kitten to the biggest lion.

3 Prime (3 - 6 years)

During this phase, your cat will literally be in the prime of his or her life. They will be very active, marking out and defending territory without you knowing it. They are also more likely to come into contact - and therefore possibly conflict - with other cats, so it's important to keep an eye on them for injuries and illnesses. This is also a vital period for keeping up with vaccination regimes and vets appointments.

4 Mature (7 - 10 years)

From the age of about 7, your cat will start to slow down a bit, so don't be surprised at this. They may feel like their work is done in terms of your territory, so will take things a bit easier. This is a time when they are most likely to put on extra weight, so it's important to keep an eye on this. Check with your vet, and change your cat's diet appropriately; a beloved family cat is easy to overfeed, which does them no favours in the long run.

5 Senior (11 - 14 years)

As the name suggests, by this time your cat would be about 70 in human terms, so think of it like that. As with people, cats can't easily leap to their feet and do what they used to; but as supremely intelligent creatures, they still need stimulation. A senior cat will sleep the day away if left to its own devices, which is possibly a sign of depression. Food games are a great way to keep your cat mentally active; these have been developed to make senior cats solve puzzles in order to find their next meal.

6 Geriatric (15 + years)

It's not that unusual for many cats to live to this ripe old age, which in human terms would be 90 years and upwards. Don't expect too much of your beloved feline friend by this age, but don't let it go to seed, either. You'll need to watch carefully for sores and unusual behaviour, especially more frequent toilet use. Keep in touch with your vet at all times.

Size and weight

A s cats are often self-contained, independent creatures, it can be easy to think they are looking after themselves and you don't need to worry about them getting fat. In fact, your cat's weight is very important, as carrying more weight than it should will affect its joints, heart and cardiovascular system, as well as making it vulnerable to diseases like:

- Arthritis / joint problems
- Diabetes
- Pancreatitis
- Skin sores.

You will be able to give it the right amount and type of food, but you may have to be careful of adding treats, especially if you have children in the house.

Cat sizes and weights don't vary as much as those of dogs. As we will see throughout this guide, breed plays a large part in these factors. The smallest breeds can weigh as little as 5 pounds (2.2 kg), while the biggest come in at 25 pounds (11kg). As a rule of thumb, the average sized domestic cat should weigh about 10 pounds (4 - 4.5 kg).

Your vet will provide you with a weight chart, which you should consult when weighing your cat every few months. In the meantime, keep a look out for any obvious signs, like lethargy or a sagging belly. Similarly, if your cat is underweight, its ribs and shoulder blades will start to show, and be noticeable when you stroke and play with him or her.

Tonkinese

The Tonkinese is known as the "Tonk", a short haired cat with a moderate body type, which is solid and strong. Its coat consists of stiff, straight hair, which gives it a silky look and feel. Its three coat patterns are Mink, Pointed and Solid, and the cat comes in a range of eight colours. People often choose the Tonk for its striking, light blue aquamarine eyes, although this eye colour also varies from a light, golden green to a much deeper violet.

Short history

The Tonkinese is the result of crossing the Siamese with the Burmese. Siamese cats are noted for their shrill sounding meows, but the resulting cross with the Burmese means that the Tonk has a much friendlier voice, without losing any of either breed's smooth, silky coat and striking good looks. The mother breed of the Tonk is the Chocolate Siamese, which dates back to the 14th Century. The Tonkinese itself received Cat Fanciers Association recognition in 1984.

Personality

Highly mentally active, and requiring stimulation as much of the time as possible. Tonks look a little mysterious, but don't let this put you off; they are looking to you for an interesting challenge, to pit their wits against yours. They will also appear on your shoulder with surprising agility and silence, just to say hello. They like to be acknowledged, so don't ignore them, and get the family into the habit of saying hello too. Tonkinese only really thrive when they feel fully included in family life, and will suffer mentally and emotionally if this doesn't happen.

Health

Tonkinese are generally healthy cats, but are prone to certain genetic diseases, as is any cat. With the Tonk, the one thing to look out for is obesity. They like to live a life of luxury, and love welcoming people into the home; however, their personality and looks make them very easy to overfeed. Tonks can become, and stay obese very easily, so you'll have to discipline yourself and your family regarding meal times, the correct food, and very few treats.

Care

Tonks are very sociable, so you shouldn't leave them alone too much of the time, as they will scratch and damage your furniture and possessions. Take care to feed them correctly, following guidelines from your vet to the letter. Tonkinese are prone to perio disease, a gum problem which can lead to tooth loss if not kept on top of. Clean your Tonk's teeth carefully as prescribed by your vet, and schedule a regular hygienist's appointment.

Grooming

Grooming a Tonk is pretty easy, as their hair is quite short and doesn't tangle. A good weekly brushing will keep their coat in pristine, shiny condition. Also, trim the nails once a week while you're grooming, and look into their ears to see if they need cleaning out. They may not, but it's always best to check for dirt, scratches, bites and mites.

Children and families

Tonks are fine with children, as long as they are not treated roughly as a kitten. They are highly intelligent cats, so get your kids involved with games and puzzles to interact with your Tonkinese, and help their own development at the same time. Tonks love getting involved in kids games like hide and seek, as they love to feel part of the family, and like to be the centre of attention. Tag is another favourite, and Tonks are surprisingly good at fetch.

Family friendliness

You should socialize your Tonkinese with everybody in the home as soon as possible. Get both cat and people acquainted, so the Tonk gets used to faces and voices. You'll be surprised at how well a Tonkinese can recognize who's in the house, and your kids especially will love them. Expect a Tonk to appear on the breakfast bar while everyone's eating breakfast, pressing itself against your arm so you can enjoy the feel of its lovely coat. If socialized early and properly, your Tonk will be a true family friend, and any guests who come to your home will be thoroughly impressed, as Tonks love to show off to strangers.

General health

A Tonkinese, like most cats, will look after its own cleanliness and general health. The average life span for a Tonk is between 13 and 18 years, if they're neutered and looked after properly. As stated above, the two things to look out for are obesity and perio disease. Maintain a healthy diet regime, and get your family to stick to the right treats, so that the risk of weight gain is kept to a minimum. Weigh your Tonk regularly, and speak to your vet if you're worried. Periodontitis can be avoided with the right tooth cleaning routing and products, so start this when they are very young to get them used to it.

Ease of grooming

A good brushing once a week will be the most your Tonkinese will need. Their hair is smooth and fairly short, so will not tangle or get matted. Use the type of brush recommended by your vet, and get your Tonk into the routine of being groomed at the same time and in the same place every week. They love to be stroked, so grooming is just an extension of this. Don't be rough with them, but take your time and let them enjoy it. Teach other family members how to groom properly, and maybe work out a rota so somebody different gets to do it each week.

Intelligence

Tonkinese are noted for their intelligence, probably above all other personality traits. They need mental stimulation, so talk to your vet about getting puzzle games for them to play; ideally involving you and the family. Being both sociable and intelligent means Tonkinese can't go very long without some sort of contact and mental stimulation, so make sure you have the time and people to provide this. A fully happy and involved Tonk will surprise and thrill people with the things it is able to remember and recognize; it will also try and challenge you, perhaps by hiding something it knows you use a lot.

Other pet friendly

Tonks are fine with other cats, and dogs if they are properly introduced. Your Tonkinese won't cause you any problems with other pets, as long as you socialize it early and well enough. The Tonk wants to get on with everybody and everything, so let it. Just remember not to exclude it from anything that's going on in the family, as it will feel unwanted.

Playfulness

A graceful cat, the Tonkinese likes to play nice, and will mesmerize small children by its presence, before purring and snuggling up to say hello. Like all cats, it should never be treated roughly, especially when a kitten, as it will scratch and bite if put under pressure. Keep nails short at all times; but apart from this, the Tonk is a playful cat which loves to learn, and will positively help children to develop. A Tonkinese will also keep you sharp as an adult, by playing games with you while you're not looking.

4.5
out of 5

Turkish Van

The Turkish Van is a medium to long haired cat, mainly white with splashes of colour around its ears, the top of its head, back of the neck and most of its long tail. Its coat is luxurious and smooth, yet it has a sturdy body, and is strong and compact. The Van is famous for liking swimming, or at least a love of water, and is a tougher character than its luxuriant looks would seem to suggest. For all that, it loves to be with people, and will curl up in your lap.

Short history

The name Turkish Van refers to the region of Van, which is now in Turkey, but is historically part of Armenia, and has thousands of years of history, much of which is included in the Bible. Mount Ararat is in the vicinity, and the Van cat has associations with the Flood which saw Noah's ark end up on that mountain when the flood subsided. This explains the Turkish Van's love of water in local traditions, and the splashes of colour which punctuate its white coat are said to be the touches of God, in all three of the Jewish, Christian and Islamic faiths. The breed was late in being recognized in the USA, as it did not enter the country until 1982.

Personality

The Van is very friendly, but has an almost human personality. He or she will make friends with all your family, but will be unable to avoid picking favourites eventually. They really do love water, so if you have a pool, you'll have to keep an eye out. They also like to see what's going on, so don't be surprised if you find your cat on the top of a wardrobe or on the edge of the roof. They don't like being picked up, as they are robust and self-reliant. They have a sense of mischief, but never mean any harm.

Health

The Van is a healthy and active cat, which will benefit from being able to get out and about. It is prone to a type of heart disease called hypertrophic cardiomyopathy, a chronic condition which your vet will be able to diagnose easily. Whether this is genetic or not is still a matter of debate, so don't expect your Van to develop it. Ask your vet which signs to look out for, but don't worry about your cat's health generally. A good diet and access to exercise will see most Vans live a long and happy life.

Care

The Turkish Van has a one layer coat, unlike other breeds which have a dense inner coat to keep them warm. Its hair is relatively long, but is quite easy to groom, as long as you have the right brush; a slicker brush is the best type, which your vet will be able to provide you with. Also, clean your cat's teeth daily if you can, using the right brush and products. The Van is essentially an indoor cat, so details like its teeth, ears and paws should be checked regularly, and you should wipe the corners of its eyes free of matter every day.

Grooming

Although the Turkish Van looks white, it is in fact a piebald cat which has a large amount of white hair. This may seem confusing, but it's important because you shouldn't expect your Van to gleam with whiteness when you've groomed it. If you want to show it, you may want to look out for the various colours which Vans display; these range from tortoiseshell to blue, with many variations in between. Its hair is longer around the edges, namely the paws, belly and neck, and its tail is a work of art on its own, so give it extra attention.

Children and families

Vans are always top cat, especially the males, who are deceptively powerful and can be frightening to other cats, and even dogs. This doesn't mean they're antisocial, however; but they must be socialized correctly, and other pets and people introduced to them appropriately. Children love playing with Vans, as they are responsive and clever. They like to fetch, so get some teaser toys which they'll enjoy bringing back. Dogs are no problem for Vans, as long as the dog is cat friendly. Again, remember that your Turkish Van is the main pet in your household, and everyone else is a visitor.

Family friendliness

You will find that your Turkish Van dominates your family ambience, even if he or she isn't actually in the room. Children love Vans because they love to play, and Vans are good for young children because they stretch them mutually. The only thing to remember is to never let anyone pull your Van's tail, as it is its pride and joy, and anyone touching it might get a nasty surprise. Vans are extremely intelligent and perceptive, so the more you and your family can interact with them, the better.

General health

Male Turkish Vans are quite a bit bigger than females, so the weight range is between 10 and 18 pounds. In this sense, they are very much like lions and lionesses, so they really can look after themselves. This is an ancient breed, and a very strong one, but is also best kept within the confines of your home. Some of the cats are susceptible to heart disease, but this may be because of the introduction of other gene lines into their own. You should expect at least 13 years of companionship from your Turkish Van.

Ease of grooming

Although a relatively long haired cat, the Turkish Van is actually quite easy to groom. Its single layer of hair means that the right brush and technique are all you really need. They appreciate being groomed, and are proud of their coats, including the feathered areas around the belly, neck and legs. Their tails, however, are their pride and joy, so be careful how you handle them. Never pull a Van's tail, and when you're grooming it, give your cat plenty of warning. It does find some of its own rear areas difficult to reach, so will appreciate your efforts.

Intelligence

It's probably that the Turkish Van is one of the oldest living domestic cat breeds, having lived with humans for many thousands of years. As such, this cat is used to people and their behaviour, and will play its part in your household as it sees fit. You will find a Turkish Van to be more of a custodian of your home than most other breeds, who will sometimes seem to know what you're thinking. For people with young children, the Van is something really special to have around the home, which will provide your kids with stories to take to school.

Other pet friendly

Turkish Vans are fine with other pets, as long as they are introduced properly. Always remember that a Turkish Van is the alpha pet in your home, and you'll be fine. If you have more than one Van, you'll need to introduce the second one gently. Don't bring cat-hating dogs into your home, as the Van will attack them. Cat friendly dogs, on the other hand, are fine, as long as you bring them in under control. Once introduced, your Turkish Van will be friendly to every human and animal with its territory.

Playfulness

Turkish Vans understand people, from young to old, so are perfect playmates. They understand that children need to be helped to learn, and they will do just that. You may be surprised at how instinctive they are, and how they can use their own intelligence to play with people. Games that involve hiding special objects are a great favourite, and you may feel like it's the cat playing with you sometimes, rather than the other way around. The only thing to remember is to never allow anyone, however young or old, to pull your Turkish Van's tail.

4 out of 5

5

Himalayan

Known as the Himmy, the Himalayan is a long haired cat which comes in many colours, and combines the grace of a Siamese with the sweetness of a Persian. They are small, compact and big boned, but easy to care for and very fond of people. A superb family pet, the Himalayan won't get in your way, but will be watching you when you come home, and ready for a snuggle or some attention, whether that's for you or itself. Himmys have beautiful eyes and a lovely voice, so you and your family will be unable to resist their charms.

Short history

The Himalayan was specifically bred as a colourpoint cat, with a lighter coloured body and dark features. In the case of the Himmy, this colour contrast really highlights their striking Siamese eyes, which can dazzle you with their stare. The angled, still eyes have the striking sky blue of the Siamese, and stand out in stark contrast to their dark faces. Unlike the Siamese, the Himmy has a long and luxuriant coat, and a more compact, strong body shape, thanks to its Persian cross breeding ancestry. Both of these ancient Asian breeds combine to startling effect in the Himalayan. The breed was developed in the 1930s, and gained recognition in the 1950s.

Personality

Apart from their coat, the reason people love Himalayans is for their personality. This is largely inherited from the Persian, rather than the Siamese, and it is an extremely friendly one. Himmys love being with and around people, so they make perfect family cats. They are also intelligent, and will occupy themselves with toys if you buy ones which keep them interested. They are by no means demanding cats, but you should be sure you can give them the time they deserve. A Himalayan will bring something to your household which you can't put a price on.

Health

Himmys are flat faced cats, which means they are prone to breathing difficulties. They also suffer in the heat, as their faces soak it up and they are not easily able to pant enough to get rid of the excess warmth. As well as this, Himalayans are prone to a kidney disease called PKD, where cysts develop on the organ from as early as 12 months old. Vets are able to access new technology to diagnose this condition, and a responsible breeder will be able to tell you whether your Himmy's mother and / or father have the PKD gene.

Care

The most important thing to remember about caring for a Himmy is to keep her or him cool. If you live in a hot climate, you should keep your pet in an air conditioned room, especially if you are going to be away for even an hour. Himalayans can overheat quite quickly, so you shouldn't have one if there's a likelihood of this happening. Apart from this issue, Himmys are generally healthy, but you should bear in mind the general cat caveat of watching their weight. A Himmy will gain weight quickly if fed excessively, or given lots of treats.

Grooming

The Himmy is a long haired cat, so you'll have to be able to devote your time to grooming it every day. You'll need a steel comb, with fairly narrow teeth. They love being groomed, so don't worry about it. Take the comb through their coat, especially in the areas which attract dirt and grease, which they can't reach to groom themselves. You will also need to bathe your Himalayan, so introduce them to this experience when they are at the kitten stage. Some Himmys tear up a lot, so pay attention to the areas around their eyes.

Children and families

Himalayans get their personality from their Persian ancestors, which means they are placid and easy going. They will probably let you dress them up and do other things, but they won't really like it. If you want to connect with your Himmy, give them something to capture their attention, as they are deceptively intelligent cats, which is a hand me down from their Siamese mothers and fathers. You will never have any trouble from a Himmy, but if you really want to to make the most of them, keep them engaged with your household, and especially yourself.

Family friendliness

The Himmy is an extremely friendly and versatile cat, who will take in the surroundings and adapt to who's there. In this way, they are one of the most family friendly cats out there. If you live on your own, or you have a big, noisy family, the Himalayan will be perfectly happy. They like to be in charge, so let them think that. They will want the attention of everyone in the room, but that won't be a problem because they are absolutely adorable, and everybody's eyes will automatically turn to them. Definitely the centre of attention, and rightly so.

General health

The Himmy is one of the longest lived domestic cats in the world, with an average lifespan of 15 years. They are prone to two illnesses; Polycystic Kidney Disease (PKD) and respiratory problems due to their flat faces. However, you can screen for PKD, so if yours doesn't have the gene, it won't get the disease. With the right attention from yourself, breathing problems shouldn't affect your Himalayan either, as you will keep your cat in the right environment. Once these two problems are eliminated, your Himmy will live a long life, as they are robust and really quite tough little cats.

Ease of grooming

Himmys are easy to groom, but they do need to be well maintained, for their own and your sake. Cut their nails once a week, and clean their teeth at least three times a week. Pay special attention to the area around their eyes, which are their most striking feature. Being flat faced, they produce a lot of tears, so gently wipe away the matter at least once a day. Comb their hair daily with the appropriate type of stainless steel comb. Bathe your Himalayan at least once a week, to keep them smelling their best, and make the most of their beautiful coat.

Intelligence

Himmys are deceptive in quite a few ways, as they look so good. However, behind those captivating eyes is a brain which needs stimulating, so don't neglect it. They thrive on people's company, but also love to solve puzzles, so buy some appropriate puzzle toys as recommended by your vet. They are not demanding cats, so it's up to you to remember their mental requirements. If you're going to be away for hours on end, leave them some puzzles to solve with rewards at the end. Easier still, make sure your Himalayan always has the benefit of intelligent human company.

Other pet friendly

The Himmy is fine with both people and animals, as long as you are considerate in the way you introduce them to your home. Remember, your home is also home to your Himalayan; they really should be put first before you allow strangers in. The Himalayan doesn't feel threatened by anything, so won't cause a fuss with other cats or dogs. If you already have pets, you need to introduce your Himmy kitten as soon as possible, well before they are 6 months old. They will accept being down the pecking order, but only if they grow up knowing this.

Playfulness

The Himmy likes to play, but not play rough. They are rewarding, and feel rewarded themselves, when the games involve cleverness; like finding things which have been hidden, or working out what goes where. In this way, they are perfect companions for young children, as they will help with a child's development. They don't mind boisterous company, but don't expect them to put up with being used as a punchbag; they are strong, capable cats and will get out of the way of aggressive people or pets very quickly. They always know what's going on, so they will find you before you know they're in the room.

4.5 out of 5

6

American Shorthair

The American Shorthair is a particular version of the shorthair or tabby cat. These are probably the most famous cats, at least in the Western world, as they have a stripey, almost tigerish colouring. They are really people cats, who will make you fall in love with them as a matter of course. What separates the American from other shorthairs is that you can predict what colour their kittens will be. People make the mistake of thinking these cats are fat; they are not. They have a dense coat which protects them from all weathers, and make superb robust, friendly family pets.

Short history

The American Shorthair, or just shorthair as they're known in America, came to what is now the USA on British ships, where they were valued for their superb capability to kill rats and mice. This is exactly what they did when they landed in the colonies, and have been much beloved of American citizens ever since. The American is now recognized as a pedigree breed, because of its large head and full on appearance. They have also been bred to look cute to humans, which is exactly what they do. Behind that sweet smile is a powerful set of jaws. The American Shorthair was recognised as a separate breed in 1966.

Personality

The Shorthair is a sociable cat, which has been especially bred to help humans. They like to be useful, and love to be trained, so in some ways they're quite like a dog. They love being handled, as they like human company, and will tell you as much by giving you a gentle half bite to say hello. Other than that, they communicate with their expressive faces, including eyes which seem to wink at you like your uncle would. The Shorthair is a hunter, so he or she will love puzzles and games which involve a chase of some kind, with a reward at the end.

Health

American Shorthairs are tough, healthy cats, with none of the breathing or overheating problems other pedigrees suffer. It is no surprise that they have the longest lifespan of any domestic feline; 20 years. One thing they are vulnerable to is Hypertrophic cardiomyopathy (HCM), where the heart muscle thickens and becomes less efficient, leading to pain and many other health problems. You can avoid this by buying or adopting from people who have had the Shorthair tested for the disease and cleared. If a breeder or other custodian hasn't had the check done, don't take the cat on.

Care

This is an easy one. The American Shorthair is probably the easiest cat to care for in the world, as it does the job itself. It is a vigorous, muscular and well built cat, who can look after itself in any situation. Don't overfeed it, or it will become obese; but your vet will give you good advice on these issues. If you have a Shorthair which hasn't been checked for HCM, you'll need to be on the lookout for shortness of breath or listlessness, which are not something the American Shorthair would ever suffer from normally.

Grooming

The Shorthair actually sheds quite a lot, because it has guard hairs which protect its softer inner coat. If you push your hand against the nap if its fur, you'll probably find that quite a bit of hair comes away. This is because its coat generally is very dense. All you need to do to groom it is use a stainless steel brush once a week, and make sure you get into all the difficult areas. Check the ears for dirt build up, and trim the nails every 10 days or so. Apart from that, you're good to go.

The American Shorthair is perfect for families, or individuals. You need to socialize them as soon as possible, so they get used to faces and voices; but this is standard practice for any cat. Once familiarized, your Shorthair will be very much a part of the family, in an almost human way. If you have kids, they will probably fight each other to gain your cat's attention, although the Shorthair itself will calm the situation down. They do love to hunt, so get your kids involved in those sort of cat games as often as possible.

Family friendliness

The American Shorthair has no preference for age or anything else when it comes to the family environment. He or she will want to get to know everybody individually, but will also appreciate the dynamic of the group as a whole. You will find that your Shorthair actually makes your family work as a unit, and you'll miss them when they're not there. They'll comfort the elderly or sick, as is in their nature. They will also rub along nicely with guests, and bring their curiosity to the table, among other things. Involve your family with their training, from day one.

The American Shorthair is clear of the afflictions which affect other pedigree breeds, as it has a practical build and face shape, so it can breathe easily and use its muscular frame as it sees fit. No breed of cat is completely free of health issues, and one thing you will have to look out for is obesity. These cats are easy to overfeed, as people love them, especially children. Keep a careful check on your Shorthair's weight, and liaise with your vet as to what to expect as your cat ages. Generally, your American Shorthair will have no health problems.

Ease of grooming

American Shorthairs are easy to groom; just run your fingers through their coat and you'll find they shed a lot of long, guard hairs. These are there to protect the down hairs which keep the cats warm, but don't grow long enough to get matted like some other pedigree breeds. Take a comb to you Shorthair once a week, and bathe them afterwards. They like being groomed, as long as you've socialized them properly as kittens (before 6 months old). Trim their nails every 10 days or couple of weeks, and check their ears for dirt build up. Simple.

Extremely intelligent, the Shorthair is a ratter, or a hunter as is the modern parlance. They instinctively look for pests to kill, as is their duty in your family as far as they see it. They love solving puzzles, and there are some excellent puzzle toys available (ask your vet) which make the best use of their intelligence. They are generally good tempered cats, but they will want stimulation as often as possible. If they get bored, they're likely to fall asleep, which in the long term is not something you should want to happen on a regular basis.

Other pet friendly

The American Shorthair is one of the most other pet friendly cats you could ever have, as it expects to live among families with other cats or even dogs. If you have a dog which likes cats, you'll have no problems with your Shorthair; they're not frightened by or threatened by dogs, whatever the breed or size. Be careful how you socialize your animals, because an American Shorthair will challenge and beat a dog in any fight. Once you've introduced your Shorthair to other animals, however, they'll be the star of the show, and move in and out as they see fit.

Playfulness

Your American Shorthair will play with anybody or anything, no problem. They have the intelligence to know when they're dealing with a toddler, baby or elderly person. They are not rough, but remember to cut their nails, as they are strong cats with powerful paws and muscles. They should be supervised with very young children, simply because of their strength and speed of reflexes. Once socialized, your Shorthair will want to play at any time, to test itself and you. They are pleasant, easy going cats, as long as nobody pulls their tail or tugs their ears.

5 out of 5

7

Chartreux

The Chartreux is a beautiful cat, with a luxuriant blue grey coat and copper coloured eyes. It's a fairly small breed, but surprisingly well built in its frame, which contrasts with its spindly looking legs. In actual fact, the Chartreux is perfectly balanced, and was partly bred to be a "mouser"; a cat that jumps on mice from above before they know what's coming. These cats are also born to be in the human lap, and you will love stroking their medium length, thick double coat. As the name suggests, they were bred in France, and have a distinctly French air about them.

Short history

Chartreux is an abbey in France, and the name of the cat is said to relate to the Carthusian monks who run that abbey. Whether true or not, their ancestry dates back to at least the 18th Century, when they became popular with pilgrims and other visitors to the abbey. They are certainly perfect mousers, and have been bred for that purpose, so the monk theory might have legs, as it were. The breed itself first appeared at a show in 1931, and received the recognition of the USA's Cat Fanciers Association in 1987.

Personality

The Chartreux is playful by nature, and loves to please people. They are perfect lap cats, so they will be in your lap almost as soon as you've sat yourself down. If you stand up and walk about, your Chartreux will probably follow you. Bred as a mouser, the cats love to hop and jump about, to keep their skills sharp. They are very intelligent cats, so will need mental stimulation as often as you can give it. For friendliness, it's best to meet both the Chartreux's parents before you commit, as this will give you a good indication as to personality.

Health

The Chartreux is a generally healthy cat, which likes to keep fit by jumping on things. Unlike some cats which can be a bit sluggish, the Chartreux is more like a ballet dancer, albeit with a large body. They are vulnerable to the cat ailment of Polycystic Kidney Disease (PKD), and their urinary tract is quite compact, which makes them prone to struvite stones, which is excruciatingly painful for them. Your dealer or adoption agency should be able to give you a guarantee of their health in both these regards, so don't take a Chartreux on without checking first.

Care

The Chartreux is not particularly difficult to care for, as it is a robust little creature which generally keeps good health, apart from its susceptibility to the two diseases described above. Take advice from your vet as to what to feed your Chartreux, and stick to this diet at all times. Obesity is the scourge of just about all cats, and the Chartreux is no different. Give kibble treats sparingly when teaching them tricks, but don't be tempted to overfeed them. Regular grooming and vets appointments will see your Chartreux keep you company for 12 to 15 years.

Grooming

When grooming a Chartreux, it's important to remember that they need combing, not brushing. They have dense fur, which includes a thick undercoat. They shed this twice a year, so you'll find a lot of fur comes out on the comb; make sure you groom your cat once a day while this is happening. When it's not moulting, once a week with a comb should see your Chartreux keep its good looks. Trim its nails once a week, and clean its teeth once every day or so to keep its gums healthy. Also, keep regular dental hygiene appointments.

Children and families

Chartreux love being around people in general, and children in particular love their antics. They are essentially lap cats, so they'll want somebody's lap to sit in. Obviously, you should supervise very small children around your cat, but when the child gets old and big enough to house a lap cat, you can be sure your Chartreux will be right there, and your kids will love being able to stroke them and their lovely long coats. Your children will probably be jealous of their attention, but your Chartreux will keep everybody happy by rationing out its attentions.

Family friendliness

Your Chartreux will make sure he or she is very much established in your family, however big it is. They are people oriented cats, who take their own duties very seriously; remember, they were bred to rid buildings of mice and other pests, which in earlier times was a vital job. They like to please people, and are very perceptive, so you and your family are in good hands as far as your Chartreux is concerned. Always socialize your kitten as soon as possible, and get her or him used to being stroked and talked to.

General health

The Chartreux is a generally healthy cat, although not as long lived as some other breeds. Its body shape is one of long, thin looking legs and a heavier torso, which is the result of its breeding as a mouse catcher. As you should buy or adopt a Chartreux with a clean bill of health, you won't have to face it getting PKD or stones in its urinary tract. If either of these start to manifest themselves, your Chartreux will let you know soon enough, so it's worth listening to them in case they get into any distress or pain.

Ease of grooming

The coat of a Chartreux is a wonderful thing, with a blue grey tinge and plenty of folds around the neck and tops of the legs. In terms of ease of grooming, the only stipulation is you need a curry comb to make sure you separate all the hairs and remove any bits of dirt or other material. Your Chartreux likes being groomed, so this is no hardship, and will happily lie on its sides and back to give you full access. Bear in mind that they shed their undercoat twice a year, so grooming will take a bit more time, and there'll be plenty of hair to dispose of afterwards.

Intelligence

The Chartreux is an extremely intelligent cat, but it can be easy to be fooled into thinking otherwise, as they are usually very quiet. This is possibly because they were first bred in monastic conditions, so would have had to be quiet. They like to test themselves, so puzzle toys are the very best thing to buy them; any which also involve a bit of leaping or acrobatics will suit your Chartreux down to the ground. They work out the best ways to catch mice, so games which involve problem solving will be the most rewarding, for them and you.

Other pet friendly

Chartreux were bred to solve problems, including mice, but also anything else which will help their human family. For this reason, you won't have any problems with your Chartreux when it comes to mixing with other animals. They don't have a problem with dogs, and will also mix with other cats happily. They're not frightened, so don't make the mistake of bringing in some tough guy dog who thinks he'll rule the roost. As with any other cat, take time to socialise your Chartreux properly, from a very early age, and they will take care of everything else regarding other pets.

Playfulness

With their unique build and breeding history, the Chartreux are probably one of the most playful cats you could ever own. They literally seem to dance, balancing on their thin legs before jumping surprisingly high. They will also find their way into any open door, so you'll have to keep an eye on them. Your kids will love playing with them, and they will fascinate young and old for hours at a time if you want them to. Remember they are intelligent, so play which involves problem solving is the best; and don't be rough with them.

4 out of 5

8

Burmilla

The Burmilla is a medium sized cat with a long, handsome tail and a relatively small head. They are both long and short haired, and have perfectly almond shaped, big green eyes. Their coat is silver in the background, while their hairs are tipped in a variety of colours, from black to red, with literally just about every colour in between. The result of an accidental cross breeding, the Burmilla is a friendly cat with Persian roots, so is laid back but also affectionate around people.

Short history

The Burmilla traces its roots back to a rather specific date; namely, 1981. This was when somebody left a door open and a female Burmese met up with a male Chinchilla Persian, which meeting then begat four kittens, named Burmillas. These kittens had silver coats tipped with black, and seemed to shimmer when they moved. Although a random act, this new breed became very popular very quickly, and is now recognized around the world as an Advanced New Breed. Since 1981 it has been crossed into a huge variety of colours, all of which are shown off to great effect by the silver colour at the base of its coat.

Personality

The Burmilla gets most of its personality from the Burmese part of its lineage, which means it likes being with people, including children, and likes the company of other cats, and even dogs. This friendliness is not always obvious when you first meet a Burmilla, as they are also part Persian, so they can seem a bit aloof, and their striking green eyes don't give much away. However, they will soon win you over by doing something specifically to make you laugh; that's how intelligent they are. They like to be able to stretch out in their own space, but you must not let them roam.

Health

The Burmilla is generally healthy, weighing in at between 8 and 10 pounds and carrying itself very well, including its rather magnificent tail. Like quite a few other cat breeds, the Burmilla is susceptible to Polycystic Kidney Disease (PKD); but a reputable breeder will be able to give you proof that your cat has been tested for this and cleared of it. Burmillas are also prone to develop allergies, which is no doubt the result of their recent incarnation as their immune system takes its time to work itself out, helped by responsible breeders of course. Burmillas typically live for 15 years.

Care

There are no particular health requirements when looking after a Burmilla, apart from being awake to its potential to succumb to allergies. This could happen at any time, so look out for any signs of ill health, like listlessness or rashes at the base of the fur. There's nothing you can do to prevent these, but talk to your vet about which allergies a cat might succumb to. This will generally result in sticking to a healthy diet, which you would do anyway. Avoid overfeeding, as Burmillas can become obese quite quickly, as they don't run around much.

Grooming

Burmillas come in both short and long haired versions, so you'll have to make a decision before you buy or adopt as to how you want to groom them. Both lengths of coat are silky and smooth, and not prone to matting, so you won't have any problems as long as you groom your cat once a week. Use a comb or a brush, and make sure every hair is given attention, so that the Burmilla's natural oils are distributed evenly to the ends of its coat. Trim the nails regularly, and inspect the ears for bits of dirt or other matter.

Children and families

The Burmilla actively enjoys being around children, which is one of the things which makes it so popular, and which has propelled it right up the charts of the cat owning world. Although the breed was accidental in being started, it turns out that they mix with children and families extremely well. They have a playful personality which makes them want to entertain people, and children especially become entranced by their little tricks. Very small children should always be supervised when animals are around, but your own offspring will take to their Burmilla chum very quickly, and love them forever.

Family friendliness

Your Burmilla will get to know every member of your family very quickly, and never cause you any trouble. They don't whine or mewl, and will keep themselves to themselves if their presence is not required. You should give them some private space where they can have some me time, as this is important to them. Think of your Burmilla as a member of the family, much like a human being. When you least expect it, they'll appear when they've got an audience and perform some trick to make everybody laugh. These cats have a lot of personality, so make the most of it.

General health

Generally speaking, your Burmilla will keep good health for the 15 or so years you have the pleasure of his or her company. The PKD they are prone to should be bred out of them, and you should know this before you buy or adopt one. As for their proneness to allergies, this is completely unpredictable, as they may or may not develop at any time. The way to best deal with this is to listen to your vet, feed your Burmilla properly and keep an eye on it. You'll soon get to know their personality, so you'll know if and when their behaviour or demeanour changes.

Ease of grooming

The grooming issue with Burmillas is slightly odd, in that these beautiful cats come in both long and short haired versions. This being the case, you'd think that long haired Burmillas would be harder to groom than their short haired cousins. In fact, they're not. The quality of the hair is the same, it's just that the long hair coat is, well, longer. Their hair is silky smooth, so you just have to make sure you comb or brush it out from the base once a week. Keep their nails trimmed, as they grow quickly; and maintain a good dental regime, in cooperation with your vet.

Intelligence

Intelligence is something the Burmilla has in spades, both from its Burmese and Persian ancestors. Both type of cat were bred to be assets to royal courts, and to impress guests on social occasions. They are both intellectually and emotionally intelligent, so bear that in mind when you're thinking of games to play or toys to buy. Speak to your vet about the best type of games for a Burmilla, which will certainly involve solving puzzles, but should also have a high element of fun. Your cat will know when something is wrong within the household, so expect an enquiring feline eye.

Other pet friendly

Burmillas will get along fine with other pets, as their breeding makes them able to cope with any situation gracefully. As long as you take the steps needed to socialize your pet with other animals, you'll have no problems with your Burmilla. They do like to have some space to call their own, so if your pet is enjoying some of this me time, don't expect it to welcome other pets with open arms. Having said that, it won't really bother them, as they have the personality to take people and pets in their stride. Altogether a graceful, pet friendly cat.

Playfulness

It's a part of the personality of the Burmilla that it has a sense of humour, part of which involves making mischief. It likes to make people happy, which it is able to do in the blink of an eye. The Burmilla will appreciate games which tests its intelligence, so puzzle games are a must. There is a bit of devilment about the Burmilla, but nothing that will cause you any problems. Just remember, you're dealing with a clever animal, which will take you by surprise sometimes. It really is like they're playing with you, which of course they are. Get used to it.

4 out of 5

9

Russian Blue

There are certain types of cat which carry a reputation, and the Russian Blue is certainly one of them. Sometimes compared to the Doberman Pinscher in the dog world, the Russian Blue is an estimable cat which has its own story to tell. It's long bodied and graceful, with a grey blue coat which has silver tipped guard hairs, giving it a silky smooth appearance. It also has huge green eyes in a triangular head, and is sure to impress anyone who gets an eyeful. The Russian Blue is a medium sized cat, ranging in weight from 8 to 15 pounds, with the males being larger than the females.

Short history

The Russian Blue is said to have originated in the northern Russian city of Archangel, just outside the arctic circle. It is a traveller, which has turned up in other parts of the world on sailing ships, and probably arrived with the Cossacks as part of their travelling party when they fought all across Asia. Queen Victoria was a big fan, having seen her first Russian Blue at the Crystal Palace in 1875. The Russian Blue's coat and body shape are similar to other short haired breeds; however, they gained their own recognition in 1912, since when they have proven consistently popular.

Personality

The Blue has something of a reserved character, so don't get one if you are impatient or your family expects immediate attention when you walk through the door. What you can expect, however, is a loyal friend who repays patience and time with real companionship. The Russian Blue will want to be by your side, as it is very much a loyal, companion cat. Expect to find your Blue beside you when you wake up, as he or she will want to be near you. They'll also be around when you're cooking, and love being combed while watching the television.

Health

The Russian Blue is a strong cat which will live with you for between 15 and 20 years as long as you look after it properly. Its face is a good shape, so it doesn't suffer from breathing difficulties, and it has a long, slim body with fine bones. What they are prone to, however, is bladder stones, so check with your breeder to see whether their mother and father have suffered from these in the past. Other than that, the only thing these cats will suffer from is obesity from overfeeding, so stick to a regime agreed with your vet.

Care

Taking care of your Russian Blue should present you with no problems, as long as you or your family members have the time to do so. They are healthy cats, and will take care of their own exercise, which will include climbing, so don't be surprised to see them looking down on you from the top of a kitchen cabinet. If you are unsure about your Blue's history with bladder stones, keep an eye out for symptoms of them, which your vet will be happy to discuss with you. Take care of your Blue's grooming on a regular basis, and feed them at the same times each day. The Russian Blue is a cat which appreciates and responds well to consistency.

Grooming

The Russian Blue's pride and joy is its luxuriant grey blue coat, which you should look after by combing or brushing it at least once a week. Their hair is quite thick, so make sure you get rid of any obstacles, although the Russian Blue grooms itself very well. Keep its nails trimmed, cutting them once a week, and look after your cat's teeth and gums; talk to your vet about how to clean cats' teeth properly and which products to use. Keep regular appointments for deep gum cleaning with your vets dental hygienist service.

You want your Russian Blue to be a friend to everyone in your family, including any children if you have them. When kids are very young, they might be tempted to grab your cat's tail or ears; don't let this happen. The Russian Blue is better suited to older children who have better self control, and who will stroke and pet them with a bit of care. They won't harm your children, but don't expect them to put up with being prodded and grabbed, especially by the tail, an occurrence which will see them disappear at remarkable speed, possibly shocking your child.

Family friendliness

Russian Blues are excellent family cats, who reward families who have the time and patience to get to know them. They are not overly affectionate, but once their affection is given, you can rely on 24 hours a day, for the rest of your cat's life. Expect a Russian Blue to make its way into bedrooms, to sleep next to family members who it hasn't seen for a while. Don't be put off by its lack of presence; your Russian Blue will know exactly who's in the house, but may be examining something through the window which needs its attention.

The Russian Blue will benefit from being correctly fed, at the same times every day, and with the right food. They are by no means high maintenance cats, who could look after themselves perfectly well if they didn't have you or anyone else as an owner. Their physical makeup doesn't present any particular problems, apart from their susceptibility to bladder stones. They love to climb and explore, so you should give them room to do this as much as possible, especially if you're going to be out for any length of time. Overall, the Russian Blue is a healthy cat which can live to 20 years old.

Ease of grooming

Grooming the Russian Blue is something ideally done in front of the television, which will give pleasure to both you and your cat. You need to groom your Blue at least once a week, but this won't be a chore. Their hair is thick, but not particularly long, and doesn't get matted easily. Take a comb or brush to your Russian Blue's coat, paying attention to the areas around the top of the legs where they themselves can't reach so well. Once you start grooming, your Blue will enjoy every second of it, so take your time and do it right.

Russian Blues are highly intelligent creatures, who will look for ways to explore and solve problems. While they can't exactly be trained as such, they can actually train you to work out ways to play with them which they themselves like. That's how clever they are. They will also work out how to fit themselves into seemingly impossibly small spaces, which may be a legacy of their travelling past. Expect your Russian Blue to challenge you to mental duels, and be ready to help them out. They are intriguing cats, and they like to be intrigued, so use your imagination.

Other pet friendly

The Russian Blue will take any visitors in its stride as long as it doesn't receive a shock. If you introduce a dog into your household, make sure it's a cat friendly dog; this is just common sense. Also, other cats won't have any trouble mixing with the Russian Blue, as it's not precious about its territory like some other pure breeds. Socialize your Blue from as early a date as possible, or at least make sure your breeder has done so. The Russian Blue will get along fine with any other pet as long as it is introduced properly.

Playfulness

One thing the Russian Blue is especially noted for is its love of feathers. It is instantly fascinated by feathers, and its attention will be rapt as soon as it sees a feathered toy. It'll try and catch it with one paw, and follow every little movement with great intensity. There are feathered toys available especially designed to keep Russian Blues occupied; combine these with problem solving and you'll have one very happy cat. Your children will also love playing with your Blue, so teach them how to use feathered toys properly and everybody's laughing, while being fascinated at the same time.

4.5 out of 5

Nebelung

The Nebelung is a long haired version of the Russian Blue. It's long bodied and graceful, with a grey blue coat which has silver tipped guard hairs, giving it a silky smooth appearance. It also has huge green eyes in a triangular head, and is sure to impress anyone who gets an eyeful. The Nebelung is a medium sized cat, ranging in weight from 8 to 15 pounds, with the males being larger than the females.

Short history

Nebelung means "creature of the mist", which is a reference to German mythology as made famous by Richard Wagner and the Ring of the Niebelungen. The Nebelung got this name because its long, blue grey coat makes it look like it's just come out of the fog. The breed was created in 1987 by crossing two Russian Blues who happened to have long coats. The result was a brood of long haired kittens, and from there the Nebelung was born. Its longer definition is the Longhaired Russian Blue, and it gained international recognition in 1997. Apart from the length of its coat, the Nebelung shares all its characteristics with the Blue.

Personality

The Neblung has something of a reserved character, so don't get one if you are impatient or your family expects immediate attention when you walk through the door. What you can expect, however, is a loyal friend who repays patience and time with real companionship. The Nebelung will want to be by your side, as it is very much a loyal, companion cat. Expect to find your Blue beside you when you wake up, as he or she will want to be near you. They'll also be around when you're cooking, and love being combed while watching the television.

Health

The Nebelung is a strong cat which will live with you for between 15 and 20 years as long as you look after it properly. Its face is a good shape, so it doesn't suffer from breathing difficulties, and it has a long, slim body with fine bones. What they are prone to, however, is bladder stones, so check with your breeder to see whether their mother and father have suffered from these in the past. Other than that, the only thing these cats will suffer from is obesity from overfeeding, so stick to a regime agreed with your vet.

Care

Taking care of your Nebelung should present you with no problems, as long as you or your family members have the time to do so. They are healthy cats, and will take care of their own exercise, which will include climbing, so don't be surprised to see them looking down on you from the top of a kitchen cabinet. If you are unsure about your Blue's history with bladder stones, keep an eye out for symptoms of them, which your vet will be happy to discuss with you. Take care of your Nebelung's grooming on a regular basis, and feed them at the same times each day. The Nebelung is a cat which appreciates and responds well to consistency.

Grooming

The Nebelung's pride and joy is its luxuriant grey blue coat, which you should look after by combing or brushing it at least once a week. Their hair is quite thick, so make sure you get rid of any obstacles, although the Nebelung grooms itself very well. Keep its nails trimmed, cutting them once a week, and look after your cat's teeth and gums; talk to your vet about how to clean cats' teeth properly and which products to use. Keep regular appointments for deep gum cleaning with your vet's dental hygienist service.

Children and families

You want your Nebelung to be a friend to everyone in your family, including any children if you have them. When kids are very young, they might be tempted to grab your cat's tail or ears; don't let this happen. The Nebelung is better suited to older children who have better self control, and who will stroke and pet them with a bit of care. They won't harm your children, but don't expect them to put up with being prodded and grabbed, especially by the tail, an occurrence which will see them disappear at remarkable speed, possibly shocking your child.

Family friendliness

Nebelungs are excellent family cats, who reward families who have the time and patience to get to know them. They are not overly affectionate, but once their affection is given, you can rely on their love 24 hours a day, for the rest of your cat's life. Expect a Nebelung to make its way into bedrooms, to sleep next to family members who it hasn't seen for a while. Don't be put off by its lack of presence; your Nebelung will know exactly who's in the house, but may be examining something through the window which needs its attention.

General health

The Nebelung will benefit from being correctly fed, at the same times every day, and with the right food. They are by no means high maintenance cats, who could look after themselves perfectly well if they didn't have you or anyone else as an owner. Their physical makeup doesn't present any particular problems, apart from their susceptibility to bladder stones. They love to climb and explore, so you should give them room to do this as much as possible, especially if you're going to be out for any length of time. Overall, the Nebelung is a healthy cat which can live to 20 years old.

Ease of grooming

Grooming the Russian Blue is something ideally done in front of the television, which will give pleasure to both you and your cat. You need to groom your Nebelung at least once a week, but this won't be a chore. Their hair is thick, but not particularly long, and doesn't get matted easily. Take a comb or brush to your Nebellung's coat, paying attention to the areas around the top of the legs where they themselves can't reach so well. Once you start grooming, your Blue will enjoy every second of it, so take your time and do it right.

Intelligence

Nebelungs are highly intelligent creatures, who will look for ways to explore and solve problems. While they can't exactly be trained as such, they can actually train you to work out ways to play with them which they themselves like. That's how clever they are. They will also work out how to fit themselves into seemingly impossibly small spaces, which may be a legacy of their travelling past. Expect your Nebelung to challenge you to mental duels, and be ready to help them out. They are intriguing cats, and they like to be intrigued, so use your imagination.

Other pet friendly

The Nebelung will take any visitors in its stride as long as it doesn't receive a shock. If you introduce a dog into your household, make sure it's a cat friendly dog; this is just common sense. Also, other cats won't have any trouble mixing with the Nebelung, as it's not precious about its territory like some other pure breeds. Socialize your Nebelung from as early a date as possible, or at least make sure your breeder has done so. The Nebelung will get along fine with any other pet as long as it is introduced properly.

Playfulness

One thing the Nebelung is especially noted for is its love of feathers. It is instantly fascinated by feathers, and its attention will be rapt as soon as it sees a feathered toy. It'll try and catch it with one paw, and follow every little movement with great intensity. There are feathered toys available especially designed to keep Nebelungs occupied; combine these with problem solving and you'll have one very happy cat. Your children will also love playing with your Nebelung, so teach them how to use feathered toys properly and everybody's laughing, while being fascinated at the same time.

11

Sphynx

The Sphynx is a very striking looking cat, which is not to everyone's taste. Basically, it looks like it has no hair, just folds of skin around its body. This is in fact not true, just that the Sphynx's coat is extremely fine, and more like down than fur. When you touch a Sphynx, you'll be captivated by how warm they feel, as the heat of their bodies comes through to the touch. Also, the feel of their downy coat is extremely pleasant, and these cats love being stroked. Sphynxes weigh between 6 and 12 pounds, and come in a huge range of colours and patterns.

Short history

The Sphynx's distinctive, hairless appearance is not the result of careful breeding, but Mother Nature. Hairless cats do occur, and examples of them have been written about for many years. The Sphynx is the result of a crossing between naturally hairless cats and the Rex breed, a process which began in the 1970s, after the very first Sphynx was bred in Toronto in 1966. Since then, breeders have been crossing the Sphynx with cats of almost all patterns, from Tortoiseshell to cream, red or blue. The cat is still carving out its own niche in the world of pet lovers and shows.

Personality

Much of the Sphynx's personality is dominated by its need to keep warm. As its coat does not retain heat, the Sphynx wants to be cuddled all the time, so if you like to cuddle cats, the Sphynx is for you. They are also naturally affectionate cats, so it's not just about the warmth; they like company, whether that's of people or other cats. You should have more than one if you're going to be out all day, so they can play together and keep each other warm. Sphynxes are known to flirt with people, so your house guests will be charmed.

Health

The Sphynx is generally a healthy cat, but is genetically prone to a couple of diseases. These are hypertrophic cardiomyopathy (HCM) and hereditary myopathy. The first is a condition in the heart, where the muscle thickens up, making the organ less effective, and leading to a number of other conditions. Ask your vet to give your Sphynx an ECG to see whether there is any HCM present. Breeders can't guarantee your Sphynx won't develop this, so don't believe them if they do. Hereditary myopathy affects the cat's nerves, which in turn stop muscles from working. This is being steadily bred out of the Sphynx line.

Care

Taking care of your Sphynx is in many ways much easier than with other breeds of cat, as you don't have to worry about things to do with a furry coat. They are prone to damage from the sun, so don't let them outside for too long. Also, you'll need to clean their teeth properly, as they are prone to perio disease, where their gums become inflamed and eventually recede. Ask your vet's advice on how to combat this, and get your Sphynx used to having its teeth cleaned properly every day. Remembrer, it's the gum line that's important.

Grooming

Grooming your Sphynx means dealing with oil. Because it is an almost hairless cat, the oils its skin naturally produces have nowhere to go. This means oil builds up on their skin, and will stain your furniture if you don't bathe your cat regularly. Your breeder should have bathed the kitten a couple of times before you take it on, but don't take this for granted. Get your new cat into the habit of being bathed once a week. The oil clogs their pores, which can lead to soreness and skin problems. Their claws also develop a waxy coating, so clean and trim them weekly.

Children and families

The Sphynx is an entertainer by nature, so your kids will love having them around. They do things specifically to please people, and make them laugh. Being such a striking looking cat, this behaviour can take some getting used to; but children do very quickly. They will also love the fact that the Sphynx will appear under the duvet every now and then, looking for warmth and some company. As long as you keep your Sphynx well groomed, your kids will be fine around them. If you let the cats get oily, this will transfer to your children, so be aware.

Family friendliness

The Sphynx fits into the family dynamic very well. It's often better to have two rather than one, and if you follow this path, you'll notice your cats appear together, to meet and greet the family as they come home. Apart from anything else, they'll be looking for someone warm to snuggle up to, and will get round to everybody eventually. They have personalities which bring families together, plus looks that are impossible not to comment on, especially when they use their big eyes on you. Expect some headfirst greetings, plus flirting when the mood takes them. Great family cats.

General health

There are a few myths about the Sphynx, largely because of its unusual appearance and fragile looking body. In actual fact, the Sphynx is a hardy cat which can live up to 14 years, so you don't need to worry that you'll break it. The important thing to remember is the care of its skin, teeth and nails, which must be looked after properly. The oil they produce builds up quite quickly, which can lead to a number of skin conditions, which nobody wants. If groomed and cared for properly, your Sphynx will live a happy, healthy life.

Ease of grooming

In some ways, grooming a Sphynx is much easier than with other cats, in that you don't need a comb, and there's certainly no chance of matting. This shouldn't give you the false impression that grooming isn't important, however. Bathing is vital, so get rid of the excess oil these cats produce. They don't particularly like being bathed, so you'll have to make it as pleasant an experience for them as possible. You should also pay particular attention to their nails and teeth, but once you've both got into a rhythm, grooming needn't be a chore, for you or your Sphynx.

Intelligence

The Sphynx has lots of intelligence, as you'll find out very quickly. They're clever cats in the way they interact with their human family; they love to entertain, and can do this in a surprising number of ways. The Sphynx will be on duty all of the time, and may make an appearance when least expected, just to keep you on your toes. Their facial expressions are almost human, so don't be surprised if it feels like you're being interrogated. They will amuse themselves, but the more puzzle toys about, the better, especially if you are going to leave them home alone.

Other pet friendly

The Sphynx appreciates the company of other animals, not least because this offers them the chance to keep warm. Expect your Sphynx to want to welcome any other pets into your home, just to check them out to start with, and then assess the chances of having a good time. If you introduce an aggressive animal into your home, expect your Sphynx to disappear to a safe distance. This doesn't mean they're not friendly, but they will wonder who the noisy stranger is. Always take care when socializing pets, and remember your Sphynx has less of a defence in terms of fur than other animals.

Playfulness

The Sphynx loves to play, as you will soon discover. Their appearance can make them look severe, or even scary, which is why it comes as a very pleasant surprise when they nudge into you with their head to say hello. They are very curious, and will look you up and down to see whether they think you're up for a laugh. And, make no mistake about it, these cats can and do flirt with people. They're just having a laugh, and will soon pick on someone to settle down with for a warm cuddle. Kids and adults of all ages appreciate the playful nature of the Sphynx.

4
out of 5

12

Ragamuffin

The Ragamuffin is a big old lap cat. Sit down anywhere, and your Ragamuffin will be right there in your lap, urging you to stroke its long, silky coat. These are long haired balls of fun, but they should never be confused with the Ragdoll, which is a separate breed altogether. The Ragamuffin loves people, and will follow you around the house, whatever you're trying to do. They are also excellent cats to travel with, unlike many other breeds, because of their fearless, outgoing personalities. Expect your Ragamuffin to be a firm family favourite for the 13 years they typically live for.

Short history

The history of the Ragamuffin is something of a mystery, as it sort of just came about by accident and experiment. They are a mix of other long haired breeds, which is what gives them their lovely, long coat. In the mix are Birmans, Persians and Turkish Angoras, as well as other long haired domestic breeds. This is where the Ragamuffin's confusion with the Ragdoll breed comes about, as they are both the result of experimentation which went on at the same time. Whatever their history, the Ragamuffin is recognized by all national and international cat fanciers associations.

Personality

The Ragamuffin is a friendly cat, which is in large part the result of having a happy, sunny personality. They are not suspicious, rather they expect to have fun every day, and love to help people do just that. Ragamuffins even make good travelling companions, which is something that can't be said for many pure bred cats. They are one of the few cats which will accept being walked on a lead, which says much about their easy going, human friendly dispositions. Expect your Ragamuffin to be the centre of attention, much to its own pleasure and that of everyone watching.

Health

The Ragamuffin is a robust, boisterous cat, which is not always obvious due to its quite fabulous coat. Wait until yours sits in your lap, and you'll realise how big and strong they are. The breed is susceptible to two diseases, both of which can be avoided if you use reputable breeders and veterinary surgeons. The Ragamuffin can develop hypertrophic cardiomyopathy (HCM), a condition which thickens the muscles of the heart. Luckily, scientists have developed a genetic test for Ragamuffins which shows this up. These cats can also develop polycystic kidney disease (PKD), which again is avoidable if you opt for genetic testing.

Care

In terms of taking care of your Ragamuffin, this will mainly consist of grooming and sticking to a healthy feeding regime. They are tough creatures who can look after themselves, but will always benefit from being properly cared for. Look after their coats, nails, eyes and ears, and give them some room to play about in. They are energetic cats, and will find ways to play, jump, climb and generally keep themselves active. Obesity is something you should guard against, and the Ragamuffin is so adorable you and your family will be tempted to please it with treats. This will soon lead to weight gain, so don't do it.

Grooming

The Ragamuffin's main talking point is its outrageous coat, which covers it from forehead to the end of its luxuriant tail. In fact, the hairs are only medium to medium-long, and are usually silky smooth. Grooming should be done twice a week, just to keep the hairs separated, as they don't really get matty. Use a stainless steel comb as recommended by your vet, and take your time to comb out all that lovely fur. Ragamuffins with Persian blood are more prone to matting, but regular grooming will keep this problem to a minimum. Also, trim their nails every 10 days, and follow a strict tooth cleaning regime to avoid perio disease.

Children and families

The Ragamuffin breed could have been designed to please children. These cats are made for kids, and will put up with all sorts of shenanigans, from being pushed around in a pram to letting themselves get dressed up in silly hats. They can be the stars of the show at kids' birthday parties, and will never lash out, as long as you have taken the care to socialize them properly when they were kittens. Having one or two Ragamuffins around the house is a sure fire way to keep your children happy, engaged and fascinated in equal measures.

Family friendliness

Your Ragamuffin, or Ragamuffins if you choose to take on more than one, will be an integral part of your family. They love children, and children love them right back, but they will also just as readily make friends with older people, which can be a great boon to many elderly adults. They basically bring joy to a household, and engage with people on an individual basis. They are lap cats, made to jump into your lap and stay there, waiting to be stroked and cuddled. There's no way anyone in your family won't fall in love with your Ragamuffin.

General health

Ragamuffins are big, boisterous cats under all that hair, so you won't have much to worry about in terms of their health. Keep their ears and eyes clean, trim their nails and groom them properly, and you should have no problems. It's not unusual for a Ragamuffin to live for 18 years or longer. You should be able to pre-test for the presence of the HCM and PKD genes, both of which are being bred out of the Ragamuffin as the years go by. They will get fat if you overfeed them, but this is true of any domestic cat.

Ease of grooming

The Ragamuffin is easy to groom, because their personality means they like the attention. Settle down in front of the television, take out your stainless steel comb, and you're good to go. The hardest types of Ragamuffin to groom are those with Persian ancestry, purely because the Persian breed has fur which can become matty. Generally speaking, however, the Ragamuffin's hair is silky and easy to comb, and probably not as long as it looks. Get into a regular routine, and your Ragamuffin will be reminding you when it's time to settle down for a family friendly grooming session. Get the kids involved if you have them, and let your Ragamuffin teach them how to do it right.

Intelligence

Part of the Ragamuffin's happy personality is that it's a playful cat. That means it's mentally as well as physically active, so make sure you have plenty of puzzle solving toys for it to play with. Involve your family with these games, and you might be surprised at how clever your Ragamuffin actually is. They get on with people of all ages, and will recognize that elderly humans appreciate different types of activity to children. Don't make the mistake of thinking your Ragamuffin is just a fuzzball; they have a lot more about them than just their lovely coats.

Other pet friendly

The Ragamuffin is a mix of various breeds, so genetically it isn't really averse to any other animal. It will easily make friends with other cats, and dogs are just as welcome as far as the Ragamuffin is concerned. It would make sense for your Ragamuffin to have a companion if you're going to be out most of the day, so maybe think about getting two kittens rather than just one. They are not scaredy cats by any means, so expect a reaction if you bring a non- cat friendly dog home. By using common sense on your part, your Ragamuffin will be perfectly fine around other pets.

Playfulness

This is probably where the Ragamuffin beats all other cats hands down. They love playing, and more especially love playing with people. They come into their own at social gatherings, and will happily take centre stage at any type of social gathering. Expect them to join you in your lap immediately, and be ready to give them attention, which mainly means stroking. They will play for hours with other cats, children or adults, and enjoy every minute. People will compete for their attention, which is another reason why it's best to have more than one Ragamuffin knocking round the house.

13

Turkish Angora

The Turkish Angora has a famous name, in that Angora is a valued pelt in its own right, although usually associated with other animals. In terms of the cat, this coat is just as luxuriant and silky, and the Turkish Angora lives up to its billing. It is a medium sized cat with a beautiful coat, big blue or green eyes, large pointed ears and a long fluffy tail. They are usually thought of as being white cats, but in fact their coats can come in calico, tabby and tortoiseshell. They weigh between 5 and 9 pounds, and live between 12 and 18 years.

Short history

The Turkish Angora is an ancient breed, having developed naturally over many hundreds of years. It is thought they originated in what is now Turkey in the 15th Century, and is a very valued cat in that part of the world. They are fine boned animals, and have a wedge shaped head, which focuses their gaze on the viewer to great effect. The Angora label is applied to a lot of cats with similar coats, but this is the only one which the Cat Fanciers Association recognises as such. They are quite noble cats, but also playful when they get to know you.

Personality

The Turkish Angora is dominant by personality, so will expect to be in charge of things when they are at home. They get along with everyone, when given their due respect, which they will demand as a matter of course. This doesn't mean they're haughty, however; expect a cheeky bump every now and then as they announce their presence. They are assertive cats, although anything but rude. The Turkish Angora is quite a stubborn cat, so it's important you don't let it get into bad habits when it's young, as it will keep these habits for as long as you have it.

Health

Generally healthy cats, the Turkish Angora has a genetic makeup which involves its eyes and ears. Blue eyed varieties of the cat which also have a white coat are prone to deafness. Not only that, there are Turkish Angoras with two different coloured eyes; in these cats, they are prone to becoming deaf in one ear. They can get about very well even if they are deaf. The Turkish Angora is also vulnerable to hypertrophic cardiomyopathy (HCM), where the heart muscles thickens and has many knock on effects. This cannot be ruled out in natural Angoras, but those which are bred specifically will come with a certificate of clearance.

Care

The most important thing to think about when caring for your Turkish Angora is not to let them get fat. People tend to over feed these gracious, beautiful cats, and their thick fur makes it hard to tell immediately if they are putting on too much weight. Take your Turkish Angora to the vets regularly to be weighed, and stick to a strict dietary regime. Look after their mental health by keeping them engaged, and don't make the mistake of leaving them alone for long periods of time. Their mental and physical health will suffer if they are neglected.

Grooming

Grooming your Turkish Angora largely consists of keeping its coat free of dirt and other obstacles. They need to be combed once a week, to rid them of dead hairs. Although they do shed hair, they don't do so excessively, unlike some other long haired cats. Their silky coats lend themselves to grooming, and the Turkish Angora itself is an excellent groomer. Their tails are plumed, and they are very sensitive about being touched around the tail. Trim their nails once a week, and make sure you help them clean their teeth, as all cats are prone to perio disease.

Children and families

If you have children, they will love having a Turkish Angora around, and the cat will love your children right back. Being ancient cats, they take in all around them, and are well used to children. Kids also like them because they are attentive, and like to help out when they can. The Turkish Angora loves to be stroked, and will make sure they are the centre of attention, so expect competition if you're trying to get your child's attention and your Turkish Angora enters the scene. They are also funny, and will find a way to make your kids laugh.

Family friendliness

Your Turkish Angora will consider itself the head of your household, which is something you should certainly encourage them to do. They are naturally assertive, and like to look down on proceedings from a high height before making their presence felt. They will also engage with your whole family, being extremely active cats. They are surprisingly agile, so may surprise people by appearing or disappearing in the blink of an eye. Just because you can't see your Turkish Angora doesn't mean he or she can't see you; they'll be keeping an eye on everyone in the family, from youngest to oldest.

General health

In terms of their general health, the Turkish Angora needs to be protected from modern things like traffic, and diseases which can be carried by other cats. This is an ancient, noble breed who can be harmed by the modern world and the creatures in it. Having said that, if you keep your Turkish Angora indoors, they'll find plenty of places to climb, hide and hunt, to keep themselves active. Look after their mental health by providing challenging puzzle games, to keep them sharp. Physically, certain types of Turkish Angora with odd coloured eyes can become deaf, but this won't affect them too much.

Ease of grooming

For a famously long haired, luxuriant cat, the Turkish Angora is probably surprisingly easy to groom. They will need to get used to you, but once they do, they'll help you as much as they can. Basically, they appreciate their own coat and like having it kept in its best condition. They're not keen on people touching their tails or ears, so do this gently, teasing out the hair on their bushy tails and checking their ears for dirt and other materials. On top of their nails and teeth, general grooming will see your Turkish Angora look and feel fine, all of the time.

Intelligence

Your Turkish Angora will help you to teach it things, like how to turn on a tap (faucet), which is something it loves to do. This is because these cats are problem solvers, who like to help out with every day glitches to make family life run smoother. It's important to keep your Turkish Angora engaged, so don't expect them to be happy if left alone for hours at a time. Ask your vet about the right type of puzzle toys and games, and get your family involved in helping your cat solve them. Overall, a very intelligent cat indeed.

Other pet friendly

When it comes to other pets, the one thing to remember is that your Turkish Angora is top of the tree. You'll need to be careful when socializing these cats, as they will expect to be number one when it comes to feline or canine competition. As long as you remember that basic rule, your Turkish Angora will cause you no problems with other pets. If you have more than one Turkish Angora kitten, they'll have to work it out themselves who gets to be head of the household; but, like socializing any other pet, this is always possible as long as it's done early enough.

Playfulness

The playfulness of the Turkish Van comes from its intelligence, and its long association with human beings. It is a cat with a sense of humour, which some people actually find quite wicked. Don't forget, these cats have been there, seen that and got the t shirt. They'll look for fun in most situations, and will be especially engaged if there are puzzles to solve. Expect your kids to want their company at all times, and just let your Turkish Angora do its thing. Don't be rough with it, and never ever pull its tail or poke its ears, and everyone will be happy.

4 out of 5

14

Burmese

The Burmese is the ancestor of many other breeds of cat, and has a character all of its own. They are sturdy, tough creatures which are also extremely good looking, and have a smooth, short haired coat which feels like silk to the touch. The male of the species weighs in at between 8 and 10 pounds on average, although 12 pounds isn't by any means unusual. The female Burmese is a little bit smaller, averaging 6 to 8 pounds; but their build means that a 12 pound female still doesn't look fat. Their original colour is a dark brown, but they now come in many more hues.

Short history

The original Burmese was the product of a particular cat, which a sailor brought to the USA in the years between World War 1 and 2, from what was then called Burma, and is now known as Myanmar. The original cat was mid brown with dark points, as in the face, which framed its pale eyes. The Burmese is a little like the Siamese, but has a stockier body altogether, and has now been bred into the whole rainbow of cat colours. The Burmese breed was recognised by the Cat Fanciers Association in 1957, distinguishing it from the Siamese and Tonkinese breeds.

Personality

The Burmese is a naturally friendly cat, who loves to please people. They make perfect family cats, and like to show off their athletic skills, to which their short, compact body lends itself. They are also aware of the power of their gold coloured, pale eyes, which stand out in sharp contrast to their dark faces. They love nothing better than being in the company of people and / or other cats, so you could say that they are definitely sociable. They don't like to be left alone, so make sure your Burmese always has company of some kind, be it two or four legged.

Health

The Burmese is a tough character, and usually keeps good health if looked after properly. Due to their breeding, however, they are susceptible to a few genetic disorders. Their heads are broad and flat, which can lead to some deformities of the skull, as well as glaucoma in the eyes. The Burmese is also sometimes prone to feline hyperaesthesia syndrome (FHS), which means they have extremely sensitive nerve ends, and flinch when touched. Some Burmese also suffer from calcium oxylate stones in their urinary tracts, which are extremely painful. A reputable breeder will be able to provide you with guarantees that none of these are present.

Care

Burmese cats are easy to care for, as they pretty much look after themselves. You should pay attention to their eyes, which are one of their stand out features, and keep the rims and face clear of matter resulting from natural tearing. They need to be groomed, as with all cats, but apart from that the main thing to remember is not to give them too much to eat. They are quite stocky little cats, and will happily eat just about anything you put in front of them. Obesity is one of the main health problems in all domestic cats, and the Burmese is no exception to this rule.

Grooming

Grooming a Burmese is really quite easy, as their coats are very smooth and look great with a little bit of attention. You should groom your Burmese once a week, using a rubber curry brush. These are flexible enough not to pull hairs out, but sturdy enough to distribute the cat's natural oils along the full depth of its coat. After you've brushed, you might want to get rid of excess oil with a clean chamois leather, as these absorb moisture perfectly. Trim the nails of your Burmese once a week, and keep an eye on your cat's ears, which can pick up dirt easily.

Children love the Burmese cat, at least partly because they sound like they're talking to them. They have a range of vocal noises they like to practise, which vary from a rumble to a whisper, with a surprising rasp every now and then. It's no surprise children find them fascinating, which they do. The Burmese temperament also lends itself to fun, and kids love playing with them like babies, pushing them around in buggies and dressing them up in funny looking hats. If you have more than one Burmese, the floor will be taken with their antics, which kids absolutely adore.

Family friendliness

Your Burmese will make it its business to be part of your family. These are beautiful cats, who know they have a power over people, and use that power wisely. Their eyes mean they can communicate with people of all ages, and they do. They are real show offs, who like to keep people entertained, whether that's a toddler or an elderly person. You can rely on your Burmese to bring your family together, as nobody ever falls out with a cat this great. Don't let them feel left out of your family, and have a friend for them if you're going to be out a lot.

A Burmese will live on average to between 16 and 18 years of age, which tells you a lot about their general health. They are surprisingly sturdy creatures, and very active. Their minds are always alert, and they look for things to do and problems to solve, so they keep themselves fit in many ways. The diseases they are prone to are to do with their skull shape and their urinary tracts, which you can avoid completely by going to a good breeder. Apart from that, look after their teeth with the appropriate dental regime as recommended by your vet, groom them regularly and you've got one healthy cat.

Ease of grooming

Burmese do shed hair, but not excessively so like some other breeds. They do not have a specific "under" coat, just lovely, silky hair, which is actually not particularly long. You'll notice this when you groom your Burmese; the hairs separate easily, and the oil from their skins finds its way easily along the length of each hair. Burmese are also so friendly that they love being groomed, and will help you do your job properly. Their faces tend to tear up quite a lot, which is really noticeable because those faces are so dark. Just clear the matter away with a gentle detergent, as discussed with your vet.

Burmese are extremely intelligent cats, who thrive on both human company and a mental challenge. They love solving puzzles, so speak to your vet about getting the right puzzle toys, which come with a low calorie, chewy reward at the end. You will need to provide your Burmese with stimulation of the social as well as the mental kind, as their minds are very sharp, and they thrive on being in company. They will improve the intelligence of your family, especially young children and older people, as they always want to do something to keep themselves and their family occupied.

Other pet friendly

The Burmese has no problem with other pets, and will not try and rule the roost like some other pedigree breeds. You will find that other animals will find your Burmese fascinating, and your cat will play on this, possibly jumping up to a high spot so other pets can't catch him or her. They are not precious, and quite willing to share your household with other animals as well as people, as they don't feel threatened by anything. After all, they're the star of the show, so why should they worry? The Burmese is one of the most other pet friendly cats out there.

Playfulness

Burmese are made for play. They like to amuse themselves, so they strut around talking to themselves as if trying to sing. This has an addictive effect on any human watching, from baby to old age pensioner, so be ready to have some fun. Because they are so intelligent, they will need to play themselves, so don't leave them on their own for too long, or their mental health will suffer. As soon as you come home, be ready for some Burmese play, which might come at you from any piece of furniture, fixture or fitting, especially those which are high up.

5 out of 5

15

Abyssinian

Known as the Aby, the Abyssinian is a very special cat, whose owners often swear they would never have any other kind of cat once they owned an Aby. They have a distinctive look which resembles a wild cat, but are in fact one of the oldest breeds of domestic cat. Their coat is ticked, with individual hairs having light and dark bands down their length. This can lead to a shimmering effect, especially in the silvered variety. The Aby first made its way into the USA in 1935, and is now a recognized breed. They have huge ears, lion like faces and big feet.

Short history

Although named after Abyssinia, a country in Africa which is now partly called Ethiopia, it's thought that the Aby actually originated across the Indian Ocean, possibly in south east Asia. They are thought to be one of the oldest breeds of cat, having developed naturally to live alongside humans. They are highly valued companions, and have evolved into entertainers, who can be trained to do things, much like a dog. In this way, they are unlike any other breed of cat, and have been valued by royal courts and palaces for many centuries.

Personality

The Aby's personality is probably its biggest asset. Put simply, these cats are a bit crazy. Sometimes known as the Aby silly an, they are always jumping about, and will climb just about anywhere in your household in the blink of an eye. They like to do tricks, and can be trained to do them, so you'll have a lot of fun with your family thinking of new feats for your Aby to perform. One thing's for certain - the Abyssinian is not a lap cat. If you want a feline companion who will jump in your lap when you sit down, don't get an Aby.

Health

The Aby is naturally very athletic, so will keep itself fit. It is, however, prone to a disease called pyruvate kinase (PK) deficiency, a condition which affects the blood. Pyruvate kinase is an enzyme in the blood which regulates the red blood cells in the way they metabolise energy. If this sounds complicated, what it actually means for the Abyssinian is that it can become anaemic, but not all the time. PK deficiency can develop as young as 6 months, or on the other end of the scale not appear until 12 years of age. Screening will tell you if your Aby has PK deficiency present.

Care

Caring for your Abyssinian largely consists of keeping their coat maintained, and occupying their tremendous brains. Apart from this, keep a look out for signs of PK deficiency if screening has shown the gene to be present. If your Aby is susceptible, signs will include general lethargy (which will be very easy to spot, as these cats are usually extremely energetic), an enlarged abdomen, pale gums and possibly jaundice. If your Aby has been cleared of PK deficiency by screening, you won't have to worry about any of this. Like all cats, don't overfeed the Abyssinian, as obesity can creep in quickly.

Grooming

The Abyssinian actually has quite a short coat, and does not shed much hair. Use a stainless steel comb once a week to tease out the hairs, and get rid of dead ones. Their nails will also need trimming, between 10 days and two weekly. Like all domestic cats, the Aby is also prone to a gum disease called periodontitis, which sets in when plaque forms between the top of the teeth and the gum. Your vet will tell you how to clean your Aby's teeth properly, and which products to use. You should also schedule a deep cleaning regime at the vets.

Children and families

Abyssinians are excellent with children, in fact they are one of the most popular breeds among kids. They like to entertain, and get actively involved with young, playful minds. Always supervise cats with babies; but very young children especially will love watching the antics of these cats, as they leap about being silly. Older children will learn from working out new tricks for the Aby to perform; they are one of very few breeds of cat who can actually be trained to do things. Along with their infectious personalities, you can expect your kids to fall in love with your Abyssinian.

Family friendliness

As well as children, the Abyssinian also delights adults, and takes delight in delighting them. There's never a dull moment with an Aby around the place, and they will certainly be the centre of attention. They will also take in everyone in the room, and get to know family members very well. Expect a challenge as well, because the Abyssinian will want everyone engaged in some sort of puzzle gaming activity. The only thing to remember is that these cats won't settle down with you in front of the TV, as they'll find it boring and soon lose interest.

General health

A very tough cat, the Abyssinian is generally very healthy, and can live for 15 years or more. They are extremely active, both physically and mentally, so you should encourage them in both of these areas, give them attention and space to move around in. The PK deficiency gene is the only likely down side to having an Aby, and bouts of anaemia will seriously lower the cat's quality of life. Hopefully, you'll buy or adopt an Abyssianian which will be clear of this genetic disease, and will enjoy many happy years with your crazy cat.

Ease of grooming

The Aby will help you when it comes to grooming time, as they enjoy it themselves. You should set up a time once a week, which your Abyssinian will remind you of, you can be sure. A stainless steel comb is all you need for its coat, as its hairs don't need brushing, but stand out of their own accord. You'll have to get your Aby used to having its teeth cleaned properly, so start this routine from a very early age. This just leaves the nails, which will need trimming at least once a fortnight. The Abyssinian has big paws, which they'll hold out for you.

Intelligence

Abyssinians are intelligent in ways that no other cat can match; so much so that they can be trained like dogs in some respects. They will let you walk them on a leash if you go about it in the right way, and will happily perform tricks to keep everyone entertained. They respond best to puzzle toys, which involve rewarding their intelligence with a low fat treat when they've successfully carried out the task you set them. They are also clever enough to train people to train them back, so just go with the flow and do what they want.

Other pet friendly

The Abyssinian is fine with other pets, as long as they are socialized together properly and are not aggressive. Expect your Aby to want to play with other pets, and take them off on adventures. If you have other pets which are not up for the Abysissian's high jinks, keep them in another room, as the cat's natural energy and intelligence will make it want to get all parties involved. You certainly won't have any trouble with dogs in your household, although the Aby does like to be the one and only cat around the place.

Playfulness

One of the Abyssinian's stand out traits is its playfulness, which you'll notice from taking it home as a kitten. The Aby likes to be the centre of attention, and will play up a storm to achieve this. Make no mistake, these cats know how to put on a show, and will do all sorts of silly things to grab people's attention. They also like to climb and explore, so you might be surprised at some of the places they manage to get into. Overall, an extremely playful cat who will bring a ray of sunshine into your home.

4.5 out of 5

16

Siamese

One of the all time, world famous cat breeds, the Siamese is unmistakable to look at, and carries itself like no other cat. They are also famous for using their vocal cords, again like no other cat, so don't get a "Meezer" if you want a quiet life. The Siamese comes in traditional and show types, and has a pointed coat; a light coloured body punctuated with points of darkness on the tops of the ears, face, feet and tail. These darker point colours now come in a range including blue, chocolate, lilac and seal, to mention just a few.

Short history

The term "'Siamese" refers to Siam, which is a country in south east Asia now called Thailand. This country has always had a royal family, and the Kings of Siam traditionally had extravagant, stylish courts, into which the Siamese cat fitted perfectly. The breed was showcased in high society in Victorian times, being given the title "Royal Cat of Siam". Since then their natural attributes have been modified so that the show and traditional actually look quite different. What remains the same is their large pointed ears, and their mesmerizing blue eyes, which manage to look regal and slightly disapproving.

Personality

The Siamese has a very intelligent, curious personality. Some people can find this a bit much, as these cats are demanding of both your time and your attention. Because they are so vocal, they will actually talk to you throughout the day, asking you questions in a language you have to work out for yourself. In return, you get a remarkable companion, some of whose traits could be compared to dogs, although that's another subject. If you leave a Siamese alone, it will find something to do, like turn your taps (faucets) on and open all your cupboards, just to see what's in them.

Health

The traditional Siamese is a robust, healthy cat, which will live an active, happy life until it's between 15 and 20 years old. The show side of the breed is developing a number of problems, partly due to the desire for it to have a wedge shaped head; the traditional Siamese has a head the shape and size of an apple. Show bred cats suffer from problems to do with their eyes, which can become crossed due to the skull shape. Some also develop a "broken" looking tail, which can't be fixed. Other problems can arise, but screening will help you make an informed choice before you buy or adopt a Siamese.

Care

If you've chosen a Siamese which is free of harmful genetic traits caused by their breeding history, you should have a generally very healthy cat on your hands, which takes only a minimal amount of caring for. Avoid overfeeding, as your Siamese will soon put on extra weight, which leads to all sorts of other problems, from arthritis in the joints to cardiovascular problems, diabetes and cancer. Follow your vet's advice on the right type of food to buy, and stick to the same times and amounts when feeding. You don't have to worry about your Siamese going outside, as they can look after themselves very well.

Grooming

Your Siamese will appreciate being groomed, and will allow you to do so at his or her leisure. Use a stainless steel comb to ease out their hairs, and distribute the natural oils along their full length. They do shed some hair, but not excessively like other cats, and their coat is quite short, so you just need to concentrate on the basics, and help with the spots your Siamese can't reach, which are very few. Do general grooming once a week, trim nails every 10 days to a fortnight, and clean your Meezer's teeth and gums regularly.

Children and families

The Siamese is very much a family cat, and as such will be protective of your children. They are surprisingly big cats, with long legs and tubular bodies, who make great guardsmen and women. They also talk all the time, so will try to communicate with kids, including babies, who will be absolutely fascinated by them. They are patient, and will let kids paw at them a bit; but this does not include their tails or ears. Never let kids pull a Meezer's tail or poke its ears; you'll get the blame, and rightly so.

Family friendliness

In terms of the family unit as a whole, you'll find your Siamese knows exactly who's who, and what your family dynamic is. They will expect a voice in your conversation, and will make themselves heard, literally. Expect a contribution from your four legged family member on all topics, as these will be given freely. Siamese also love to watch the television, and not just for the pictures; if you think it looks like they understand what the program is about, that's because they probably do. If you could understand your Siamese, they'd explain the plot to all the family.

General health

The Siamese is a robust cat, weighing in at a healthy 10 pounds, and has long, strong legs which can get it out of trouble, no problem. What health problems they increasingly suffer from are largely due to human beings, rather than the Siamese itself. If you take on a cat with a tapered face, it will have problems with its eyes, and possibly breathing. People who buy or adopt Siamese have to make a choice between sculpted good looks and the health of the cat itself. A generally healthy Siamese will only need regular grooming, nail trimming and a good tooth cleaning regime.

Ease of grooming

The Siamese is one of the easiest cats in the world to groom. Its shimmering coat takes on a life of its own, and the hairs are short and silky, so you don't have to worry about untangling any matted lumps. A stainless steel comb once a week is all you need, and the time to groom your Siamese with care and pleasure. They will talk to you all the time you're doing it, and give you a remarkably harsh stare if you do something they don't like. Get into a routine of nail trimming and tooth cleaning, and your whole Siamese grooming regime will be very easy.

Intelligence

Cats are generally very intelligent creatures; but the Siamese is intelligent in more ways than most. Get used to your Meezer talking to you, and try to understand what he or she is saying. This may sound a little odd, but you will probably be surprised at just how clever these cats are. Like other intelligent beings, the Siamese needs mental and social stimulation, so bear this in mind. They can also be taught tricks, which not many cats can manage. It is possible to get your Siamese to walk on a leash with you down the street, and look good doing so.

Other pet friendly

Siamese don't have a problem with dogs, it's just that they themselves are always top dog. If you have other pets at home, you'll need to socialize them with your Meezer properly; don't expect to shoehorn one with the other, either way. If you bring a Siamese home as a kitten, they'll get used to everyone in the house, and start talking to them. This includes other pets as well as people. Don't be surprised if your other pets defer to your Siamese; this is just the natural way of things. This is a royal cat, after all.

Playfulness

The Siamese is extremely playful, both physically and mentally. They particularly love problem solving, so buy puzzle games for them; they also love obstacle courses, as they love to test themselves against their environment. Your kids will love playing with your Siamese, and no doubt develop private games between themselves, which your Meezer will be able to predict, and always be ahead of the game. They are funny as well, once they have the situation under control, so expect the odd joke now and then. Siamese need company, so make sure they have someone or something to play with at all times.

4.5 out of 5

17

Birman

An ever present in the list of the top ten cats in the USA, the Birman combines many of the physical features of other south east Asian cats with a luxuriant, long coat and some other rather special features. It has four white feet, which stand out from its delicately coloured coat and pointed coloured features. It has striking, almost round blue eyes, which stand out against both its dark coloured face and the generally popular golden coloured coat. It also has a distinctive "Roman" nose, which finishes off its handsome features perfectly. It's also a robust, medium to large size cat, which somewhat belies its fluffy appearance.

Short history

The name Birman comes from a French phrase, Sacre de Birmanie. This was used by the French during their time in Indochina, and means the sacred cat of the Burmese (people). The breed appeared on a registry with that name in 1919; from which, the title became shortened and Anglicised to Birman. It is thought that these cats date back many hundreds, if not thousands, of years, and were chosen to inhabit Hindu and Buddhist temples due to their superb looks and striking eyes. The Birman was introduced into the USA in the 1960s, and was an immediate favourite with American owners.

Personality

The Birman is sometimes compared to the Siamese cat, mainly because of its looks, especially around the face, eyes and ears. Its personality is different to the Siamese, however, mainly because the Birman is a very calm cat, who has a soothing influence on people, especially when they jump into your lap. This doesn't mean they're a lap cat, however; they like to be active, and will find plenty to do with themselves around the house. They are extremely people friendly, but not demanding like some other pure breeds. A Birman likes to live in a harmonious household, and will help to make this so.

Health

The Birman is a large, healthy cat, which generally keeps very good health. The females weigh from 6 to 10 pounds, while the bigger males can weigh 10 to 15. They are not predisposed to any particular illnesses, having largely evolved their own natural beauty, rather than being manipulated by human breeders. This natural healthiness means the Birman will usually live for between 12 and 16 years, and not have many or any major illnesses. Like all cats, they are prone to obesity, but you can avoid this by sticking rigidly to a dietary regime as agreed with your vet.

Care

Caring for a Birman is probably one of the easiest jobs in the domesticated animal world. They need regular grooming, of course, including nail trimming and particular attention to their gums, which are prone to perio disease. This can be rectified (or, even better, avoided in the first place) with the appropriate level of care. What the Birman craves is company and stimulation, so you should look after your cat's mental and emotional health by making sure it always has company. If you're going to be out all day, you should at least make sure your Birman has another cat, or a dog, to interact with.

Grooming

Although the Birman is a long haired cat, grooming one is probably much easier than you'd think. This is because they have single coats, rather than other supposed fluffballs which have undercoats. The Birman needs to be combed once a week, with a stainless steel comb to reach all the way to the skin and out to the full length of each hair. You will need to trim their nails at least every two weeks, so they don't catch them accidentally, possibly on your furniture. Dental hygiene is also vital, so make this part of your daily / weekly / 2 weekly grooming schedule, as agreed with your vet.

Children and families

Birmans love kids, and kids in turn love them right back. They like to have human attention, and thrive when children show them as much. Kids also adore stroking their long hair, and the Birman loves to be stroked. If you have children who like to talk to your cat, you'll find that a Birman will answer back, in a rather sweet sounding voice. The Birman isn't possessive like some other breeds, and will let your children go and do their own thing without taking offence. Always make sure to trim their nails, and don't let kids pull their tails or prod their earholes.

Family friendliness

The Birman will firmly establish itself at the heart of your family. This is partly because the whole family will adore it, want to stroke it, play with it and talk to it. The Birman is well aware of its own charms, and will expect to be adored. This doesn't mean it's a diva, or expects to boss anyone around. They have such an even temperament that you'll probably find that any tensions within the family will disappear once everybody's beloved Birman makes an appearance. From toddlers to great aunts or uncles, your Birman will bring everyone together.

General health

For a recognized pedigree cat, the Birman is probably the most naturally healthy breed out there. Its superb coat protects it from all weathers, and its facial features (including its famous Roman nose) are developed to be extremely efficient, unlike some of its south east Asian cousins. Any cat can be vulnerable to regressive genes, but the truth is that these are very rare in the Birman. They are quite heavy cats, and will eat just about anything you put in front of them; this in combination with their general adorability means you'll have to keep a keen eye on their diet, to avoid obesity.

Ease of grooming

As the Birman is a single coated cat, the breed is easy to groom. Their dense hair requires the attention of a steel comb, to get rid of any bits of dirt or matter which your cat hasn't managed to remove itself. Grooming their coat once a week will ensure even distribution of oils along the length of each hair, and ensure a stunningly superb coat. They enjoy being groomed, and will welcome the attention of any family member who wants to help them out. After that, it's just a question of getting them used to having their nails trimmed and teeth cleaned; no problems.

Intelligence

Birmans have a high level of intelligence, which you should take into account before you buy or adopt one. They thrive on attention, especially when it involves games where they can get involved and help solve puzzles with the family. The Birman is also emotionally intelligent, and will use this intelligence to help people get along, with themselves included at every stage, of course. They are not demanding like some other cats, so you won't hear them complaining about being bored or ignored; however, these are things you should avoid, and try to keep your cat engaged as much of the time as possible.

Other pet friendly

If you have other pets, or if you're expecting guests who have, you shouldn't have too many problems with your Birman. They like the company of other cats, which don't necessarily have to be Birmans themselves. They'll also get along fine with dogs, as long as they are well enough behaved. Socialization is always essential when introducing cats to other animals, so take advice from your vet about this. As the Birman is an extremely sociable cat, it will want the same thing as you do; a peaceful home where people and pets have fun together.

Playfulness

Play is at the centre of the Birman's life, in one way or another. A Birman loves being stroked in your lap, but is not a lap cat as such. It will jump up and play at the drop of a hat, and try to get everyone in the room involved. It's a puzzle solver, so concentrate on cat games which stretch their intellect as well as their instincts. The Birman is by no means a demanding cat, but just remember it is always ready to play, and will want to do so every time it sees a member of the family.

18

Bombay

The Bombay is a medium sized, black cat with a soothing, friendly and gentle personality. They have extremely smooth, short haired coats, which can be deceptive because they are surprisingly solid creatures. Males are larger than females, but the weight range is between 8 and 15 pounds; that's a sturdy, strong cat which is probably bigger than it looks. The Bombay can live from between 12 and 20 years, so expect a lifetime of companionship. They are friendly cats who get on with anybody, human, feline or canine, but will expect to be head of the household in pet terms.

Short history

The Bombay has a relatively short history, the breed dating back to the 1950s, and was the result of crossing sable (black) Burmese with other short haired black domestic cats, both the USA and in Great Britain. In the USA, the black cats used were black American Shorthairs. The resulting breed has a black, velvet like coat which is the trademark of the Bombay. It has also inherited the pleasant personality of the Burmese, and the family friendliness of shorthair breeds. Since its introduction, it has proved popular with cat owners and is now a recognized breed of the Cat Fanciers Association.

Personality

Apart from their coat, the reason people love Bombays is for their personality. This is largely inherited from the Burmese, and it is an extremely friendly one. Bombays love being with and around people, so they make perfect family cats. They are also intelligent, and will occupy themselves with toys if you buy ones which keep them interested. They are by no means demanding cats, but you should be sure you can give them the time they deserve. A Bombay will get along with anyone or anything as long as they are friendly, but they do like to be Top Cat.

Health

The Bombay is generally a healthy cat, but is genetically prone to a couple of diseases. These include hypertrophic cardiomyopathy (HCM), which is a condition in the heart, where the muscle thickens up, making the organ less effective, and leading to a number of other conditions. Ask your vet to give your Bombay an ECG to see whether there is any HCM present. Breeders can't guarantee your Sphynx won't develop this, so don't believe them if they do. What they can do is perform an ECG and test for the disease. The Bombay is also prone to tearing and can have breathing problems due to its flat muzzle.

Care

In terms of taking care of your Bombay, this will mainly consist of grooming and sticking to a healthy feeding regime. They are tough creatures who can look after themselves, but will always benefit from being properly cared for. Look after their coats, nails, eyes and ears, and give them some room to play about in. They are energetic cats, and will find ways to play, jump, climb and generally keep themselves active. Obesity is something you should guard against, and the Bombay could tempt your family into pleasing it with treats. This will soon lead to weight gain, so don't do it.

Grooming

Grooming a Bombay is really quite easy, as their coats are very smooth and look great with a little bit of attention. You should groom your Bombay once a week, using a rubber curry brush. These are flexible enough not to pull hairs out, but sturdy enough to distribute the cat's natural oils along the full depth of its coat. After you've brushed, you might want to get rid of excess oil with a clean chamois leather, as these absorb moisture perfectly. Trim the nails of your Bombay once a week, and keep an eye on your cat's ears, which can pick up dirt easily.

Children love the Bombay cat, at least partly because they sound like they're talking to them. They have a range of vocal noises they like to practise, which vary from a rumble to a whisper, with a surprising rasp every now and then. It's no surprise children find them fascinating, which they do. The Bombay temperament also lends itself to fun, and kids love playing with them like babies, pushing them around in buggies and dressing them up in funny looking hats. If you have more than one Bombay, the floor will be taken with their antics, which kids absolutely adore.

Family friendliness

Your Bombay will make it its business to be part of your family. These are beautiful cats, who know they have a power over people, and use that power wisely. Their eyes mean they can communicate with people of all ages, and they do. They are real show offs, who like to keep people entertained, whether that's a toddler or an elderly person. You can rely on your Bombay to bring your family together, as nobody ever falls out with a cat this great. Don't let them feel left out of your family, and have a friend for them if you're going to be out a lot.

A Bombay will live as long as 20 years of age, which tells you a lot about their general health. They are surprisingly sturdy creatures, and very active. Their minds are always alert, and they look for things to do and problems to solve, so they keep themselves fit in many ways. The diseases they are prone to are to do with their skull shape, which you can avoid completely by going to a good breeder. Apart from that, look after the Bombay's teeth with the appropriate dental regime as recommended by your vet, groom them regularly and you've got one healthy cat.

Ease of grooming

Bombays do shed hair, but not excessively so like some other breeds. They do not have a specific "under" coat, just lovely, silky hair, which is actually not particularly long. You'll notice this when you groom your Bombay; the hairs separate easily, and the oil from their skins finds its way easily along the length of each hair. Bombays are also so friendly that they love being groomed, and will help you do your job properly. Their faces do tear up quite a lot, which is really noticeable because those faces are so dark. Just clear the matter away with a gentle detergent, as discussed with your vet.

Bombays are extremely intelligent cats, who thrive on both human company and a mental challenge. They love solving puzzles, so speak to your vet about getting the right puzzle toys, which come with a low calorie, chewy reward at the end. You will need to provide your Bombay with stimulation of the social as well as the mental kind, as their minds are very sharp, and they thrive on being in company. They will improve the intelligence of your family, especially young children and older people, as they always want to do something to keep themselves and their family occupied.

Other pet friendly

The Bombay has no problem with other pets, but will expect to rule the roost, like many pedigree breeds. You will find that other animals will find your Bombay fascinating, and your cat will play on this, possibly jumping up to a high spot so other pets can't catch him or her. They are not precious, and quite willing to share your household with other animals as well as people, as long as it's understood that they're number 1. After all, they're the star of the show, so why should they worry? The Bombay is one of the most other pet friendly cats out there.

Playfulness

Bombays are made for play. They like to amuse themselves, so they strut around talking to themselves as if trying to sing. This has an addictive effect on any human watching, from baby to old age pensioner, so be ready to have some fun. Because they are so intelligent, they will need to play themselves, so don't leave them on their own for too long, or their mental health will suffer. As soon as you come home, be ready for some Bombay play, which might come at you from any piece of furniture, fixture or fitting, especially those which are high up.

19

Scottish Fold

The Scottish Fold is a cat named for a particular feature of its anatomy; its ears, which fold forward, giving the cat a very unusual appearance. Some people liken the look to an owl, as it shows off the shape of the Fold's head, which is round, with big eyes, and round rather than almond. Folds have coats of varying length, and also a huge range of colours and patterns, making them a breed with one of the largest ranges of options in this department. They are born with normal ears, but these soon start to fold forward.

Short history

The Scottish Fold came about rather by accident, about 50 years ago, when a Scottish shepherd got his eye on a cat with folded ears, and bought a kitten from this parent. This single cat was a female, and every kitten she bore also had folded ears. Since then, the breed has been crossed with a number of pedigrees, including American Shorthairs, Burmese and Persians. Because of this history, the Fold can be outcrossed to American and British Shorthairs, but people like the folded look, and the Cat Fanciers Association have recognized the breed.

Personality

The Fold is a friendly cat, which is in large part the result of having a happy, sunny personality. They are not suspicious, rather they expect to have fun every day, and love to help people do just that, which says much about their easy going, human friendly dispositions. Expect your Scottish Fold to be the centre of attention, much to its own pleasure and that of everyone watching. They are also very dexterous, and will open cabinets or try to turn your taps (faucets) on. The Fold likes playing with water, just to see it splash and have a bit of fun.

Health

The Scottish Fold should live to about 15 years old, as it is generally a healthy, robust cat. However, they are susceptible to a few conditions. One of these is osteochondrodystrophy (OCD, and not the human kind), which is a disorder of the skeleton, and can be extremely painful for the Fold, and eventually cripple the cats. Breeders are trying to get rid of OCD in Folds, by breeding them with straight eared cats, but this will take a while. When buying or adopting a Fold, you should avoid kittens which have a short, thick tail, and very stiff legs.

Care

In terms of taking care of your Scottish Fold, this will mainly consist of grooming and sticking to a healthy feeding regime. They are tough creatures who can look after themselves, but will always benefit from being properly cared for. Look after their coats, nails, eyes and ears, and give them some room to play about in. They are energetic cats, and will find ways to play, jump, climb and generally keep themselves active. Obesity is something you should guard against, and the Scottish Fold is so adorable you and your family will be tempted to please it with treats. This will soon lead to weight gain, so don't do it.

Grooming

The Scottish Fold coat varies from short to medium to medium-long and long haired, but whatever the length, their coats are always silky smooth. Grooming should be done twice a week, just to keep the hairs separated, as they don't really get matty. Use a stainless steel comb as recommended by your vet, and take your time to comb out all that lovely fur. Longer haired Folds may get a few knots in their coats, but regular grooming will keep this problem to a minimum. Also, trim their nails every 10 days, and follow a strict tooth cleaning regime to avoid perio disease.

Children and families

Scottish Folds are excellent with children, in fact one of the most popular breeds among kids. They like to entertain, and get actively involved with young, playful minds. Always supervise cats with babies; but very young children especially will love watching the antics of these cats, as they leap about being silly. Older children will learn from working out new tricks for the Fold to perform; and they have a natural trick of standing on their back legs and making like a Meerkat. Along with their infectious personalities, you can expect your kids to fall in love with your Scottish Fold.

Family friendliness

As well as children, the Scottish Fold also delights adults, and takes delight in delighting them. There's never a dull moment with a Fold around the place, and they will certainly be the centre of attention. They will also take in everyone in the room, and get to know family members very well. Expect a challenge as well, because the Fold is clever with its paws and will helpfully try to turn things on and off for you. The only thing to remember is that these cats won't settle down with you in front of the TV, as they'd rather be playing fetch.

General health

A pretty tough cat, the Scottish Fold is generally very healthy, and can live for 15 years or more. They are extremely active, both physically and mentally, so you should encourage them in both of these areas, give them attention and space to move around in. The OCD gene is the only likely down side to having a Fold, as it is degenerative, hugely painful for them and eventually it will disable them completely. Hopefully, you'll buy or adopt a Scottish Fold which will be clear of this genetic disease, and will enjoy many happy years with your crazy cat.

Ease of grooming

The Scottish Fold will help you when it comes to grooming time, as they enjoy it themselves. You should set up a time once a week, which your Fold will remind you of, you can be sure. A stainless steel comb is all you need for its coat, as its hairs don't need brushing, but stand out of their own accord. You'll have to get your Fold used to having its teeth cleaned properly, so start this routine from a very early age. This just leaves the nails, which will need trimming at least once a fortnight. Oh, and be careful with those ears.

Intelligence

The Scottish Fold has a very intelligent, curious personality. If you leave a Scottish Fold alone, it will find something to do, like turn your taps (faucets) on and open all your cupboards, just to see what's in them. Like other intelligent beings, the Siamese needs mental and social stimulation, so bear this in mind. They can also be taught tricks, which not many cats can manage. The Fold will want to involve you and your family with puzzles and games, so take full advantage of this, and you'll find that both the people and cat in the family will thrive.

Other pet friendly

If you have other pets, or if you're expecting guests who have, you shouldn't have too many problems with your Scottish Fold. They like the company of other cats, which don't necessarily have to be Folds themselves. They'll also get along fine with dogs, as long as they are well enough behaved. Socialization is always essential when introducing cats to other animals, so take advice from your vet about this. As the Scottish Fold is an extremely sociable cat, it will want the same thing as you do; a peaceful home where people and pets have fun together.

Playfulness

Play is at the centre of the Scottish Fold's life, in one way or another. A Fold loves being stroked in your lap, but is not a lap cat as such. It will jump up and play at the drop of a hat, and try to get everyone in the room involved. It's a puzzle solver, so concentrate on cat games which stretch their intellect as well as their instincts. The Scottish Fold is by no means a demanding cat, but just remember it is always ready to play, and will want to do so every time it sees a member of the family.

4 out of 5

20

British Shorthair

The British Shorthair could be described as the British Bulldog of cats. They are muscular, tough cats who are easy to get along with once they get to know you. They have very dense hair, which needs quite a lot of attention, but this means they have coats which are really quite beautiful, and come in a huge range of colours and patterns. Also they have big, round heads and weigh in at between 7 and 12 pounds, the males especially being something to be reckoned with. British Shorthairs live to between 14 and 20 years, and you'll have a good pal with you for all that time.

Short history

The British Shorthair can trace its roots back to the Roman Empire, over 2,000 years ago. The Legions took cats with them wherever they went, to keep mice and other pests at bay. One place they took their cats was Britannia, which later became Great Britain. Sometimes known as the British Blue because of their natural colour, the breed became popular in Victorian England, and known as the Shorthair. It nearly died out during World War I, but was revived successfully, becoming crossed with other short haired cats, including Russian Blues. The Cat Fanciers Association recognized the British Shorthair in 1980.

Personality

The British Shorthair is known for smiling, which is partly how the Cheshire Cat of Alice in Wonderland fame came about. True enough, the male of the breed are happy go lucky chaps, but the smile is a genetic trait rather than an effort. Female Shorthairs have a slightly serious air about them; probably because they're worried about their male counterparts, who are frightened of nothing and nobody. They both enjoy the company of people, and will muscle their way into your family's affections, without being unpleasant about it. They're also very clever cats, who don't miss a thing, in their own quiet way.

Health

British Shorthairs are tough, healthy cats, with none of the breathing or overheating problems other pedigrees suffer. It is no surprise that they have the longest lifespan of any domestic feline; 20 years. One thing they are vulnerable to is Hypertrophic cardiomyopathy (HCM), where the heart muscle thickens and becomes less efficient, leading to pain and many other health problems. You can avoid this by buying or adopting from people who have had the Shorthair tested for the disease and cleared. They are also prone to haemophilia B; but a new DNA is helping breeders eradicate this from the British Shorthair line.

Care

This is an easy one. The British Shorthair is probably the easiest cat to care for in the world, as it does the job itself. It is a vigorous, muscular and well built cat, who can look after itself in any situation. Don't overfeed it, or it will become obese; but your vet will give you good advice on these issues. If you have a Shorthair which hasn't been checked for HCM, you'll need to be on the lookout for shortness of breath or listlessness, which are not something the British Shorthair would ever suffer from normally.

Grooming

The Shorthair actually sheds quite a lot, because it has guard hairs which protect its softer inner coat. If you push your hand against the nap of its fur, you'll probably find that quite a bit of hair comes away. This is because its coat generally is very dense. All you need to do to groom it is use a stainless steel brush once a week, and make sure you get into all the difficult areas. Take extra time in the spring, when the British Shorthair sheds its coat completely to make way for a new year's coat.

Children and families

The British Shorthair is perfect for families, or individuals. You need to socialize them as soon as possible, so they get used to faces and voices; but this is standard practice for any cat. Once familiarized, your Shorthair will be very much a part of the family, in an almost human way. If you have kids, they will probably fight each other to gain your cat's attention, although the Shorthair itself will calm the situation down. They do love to hunt, so get your kids involved in those sort of cat games as often as possible.

Family friendliness

The British Shorthair has no preference for age or anything else when it comes to the family environment. He or she will want to get to know everybody individually, but will also appreciate the dynamic of the group as a whole. You will find that your Shorthair actually makes your family work as a unit, and you'll miss them when they're not there. They'll comfort the elderly or sick, as is in their nature. They will also rub along nicely with guests, and bring their curiosity to the table, among other things. Involve your family with their training, from day one.

General health

The British Shorthair is clear of the afflictions which affect other pedigree breeds, as it has a practical build and face shape, so it can breathe easily and use its muscular frame as it sees fit. No breed of cat is completely free of health issues, and one thing you will have to look out for is obesity. These cats are easy to overfeed, as people love them, especially children. Keep a careful check on your Shorthair's weight, and liaise with your vet as to what to expect as your cat ages. Generally, your British Shorthair will have no health problems.

Ease of grooming

British Shorthairs are easy to groom; just run your fingers through their coat and you'll find they shed a lot of long, guard hairs. These are there to protect the down hairs which keep the cats warm, but don't grow long enough to get matted like some other pedigree breeds. Take a comb to you Shorthair once a week, and bathe them afterwards. They like being groomed, as long as you've socialized them properly as kittens (before 6 months old). Trim their nails every 10 days or couple of weeks, and check their ears for dirt build up.

Intelligence

Extremely intelligent, the British Shorthair is a natural pest controller. They instinctively look for rodents to kill, as is their duty in your family as far as they see it. They love solving puzzles, and there are some excellent puzzle toys available (ask your vet) which make the best use of their intelligence. The British Shorthair is a naturally calm, and calming, creature, but don't make the mistake of thinking this makes them thick. They will stay exactly where they are, usually on the floor, and appear to sleep, while in fact their ears, nose and especially whiskers are on high alert for pests or play.

Other pet friendly

The British Shorthair is one of the most other pet friendly cats you could ever have, as it expects to live among families with other cats or even dogs. If you have a dog which likes cats, you'll have no problems with your Shorthair; they're not frightened by or threatened by dogs, whatever the breed or size. Be careful how you socialize your animals, because a British Shorthair will challenge and beat a dog in any fight. Once you've introduced your Shorthair to other animals, however, they'll be the star of the show, and move in and out as they see fit.

Playfulness

Your British Shorthair will play with anybody or anything, no problem. They have the intelligence to know when they're dealing with a toddler, baby or elderly person. They are not rough, but remember to cut their nails, as they are strong cats with powerful paws and muscles. They should be supervised with very young children, simply because of their strength and speed of reflexes. Once socialized, your Shorthair will want to play at any time, to test itself and you. They are pleasant, easy going cats, as long as nobody pulls their tail or tugs their ears.

5 out of 5

21

Persian

The Persian is probably the most popular breed of cat in the entire human world. Their characteristics have been bred into other types of cat, from their coats, eyes colouring to their wonderful personalities. They have round heads, a flat face and little nose, are a medium sized cat and weigh between 7 and 12 pounds. They live from 10 to 17 years of age, and make great companions. What many people buy or adopt a Persian for, however, is their fabulous coat and entrancing eyes, which make them real show stoppers, even if they're just sitting at home waiting to be fed.

Short history

The short history of the Persian cat is actually a very long one. They've been roaming the earth for probably thousands of years, pleasing caliphs and emperors or anybody else who might feed them. Persian refers to Persia, an ancient empire based around what is now called Iran. The empire spread across three continents, and so did these cats. The Persian became extremely popular in Victorian era Britain, as did many other modern pedigree breeds. Like other pedigrees, today they come in traditional and show varieties; and like those other breeds, owners need to strike a balance between looks and their pets' health.

Personality

The Persian has a calm and soothing personality, which is a perfect antidote to the stresses of the 21st Century. They appreciate good manners, and are very good mannered themselves, although they can seem a little aloof to impatient people. A Persian will observe proceedings from a suitably high vantage point, so they can see what's going on and assess the situation. They are perfectly at home with people of any age, and appreciate that children need to be amused. The Persian communicates partly through its voice, but mainly with its eyes, which mesmerize people as soon as they walk through the door.

Health

The Persian is one of the longest lived domestic cats in the world, with an average lifespan of 15 years (they often live to be 20). However, they are susceptible to some hereditary diseases. These are Polycystic Kidney Disease (PKD), which can appear between the ages of 7 and 10 years. They are also vulnerable to progressive retinal atrophy (PRA), which appears when they are only weeks old and can make them completely blind by 15 weeks. Like many other cats, the Persian is prone to hypertrophic cardiomyopathy (HCM), bladder stones and cystitis. Choose a breeder who has had their Persian checked for these.

Care

There are no particular health requirements when looking after a Persian, apart from being awake to its potential to suffer from its genetic inheritance. This could happen at any time, so look out for any signs of ill health, as discussed and agreed with your vet and breeder. There's nothing you can do to prevent these, but genetics, not withstanding, your Persian should be able to live a long, happy and healthy life. This will always depend on sticking to a healthy diet, which any responsible pet owner will always provide. Avoid overfeeding, as Persians can become obese quite quickly, as they don't run around much.

Grooming

The one thing about Persians is that they need a lot of grooming. The Persian needs to be groomed every day, so don't think about getting one unless you or other people can commit to this. You'll need a stainless steel comb to separate its long, luxuriant hairs, which are prone to matting and knotting. The Persian itself is unable to prevent or deal with these problems, so you as an owner will have to. They shed a lot of hair, which will soon become clear throughout your home. Some types of Persian have silky coats, while others have hair which is more like cotton.

Children and families

Persians have a long history of living with children, thanks to their ancestors; this means they are placid and easy going. They will probably let your kids dress them up and do other things, as long as you teach your children not to be rough with them; particularly not to pull their tail or poke their ears. Apart from that, your Persian will love your kids, and vice versa. You'll certainly never have any trouble from a Persian, but if you really want to make the most of them, keep them engaged with your household, and include your children whenever possible.

Family friendliness

The Persian is an extremely friendly and versatile cat, who will take in their surroundings and adapt to who's there. In this way, they are one of the most family friendly cats out there. If you live on your own, or you have a big, noisy family, the Persian will be perfectly happy. They like to be in charge, so let them think that. They will want the attention of everyone in the room, but that won't be a problem because they are absolutely adorable, and everybody's eyes will automatically turn to them. The Persian is always the centre of attention, and rightly so.

General health

The Persian is one of the longest lived domestic cats in the world, with an average lifespan of 15 years. They are prone to the illnesses listed above, including Kidney Disease (PKD), progressive retinal atrophy (PRA) and respiratory problems due to their flat faces. However, you can screen for more and more diseases today, so if your Persian doesn't have the gene, it won't get the diseases. For many owners of Persians, their personality, looks and beneficial effect on family life overrule these potential health problems; although obviously you don't want your pet to suffer from avoidable illnesses and health complaints.

Ease of grooming

Persians are easy to groom, but they do need the time to be well maintained, for their own and your sake. Cut their nails once a week, and clean their teeth at least three times a week. Pay special attention to the area around their eyes, which are their most striking feature. Being flat faced, they produce a lot of tears, so gently wipe away the matter at least once a day. Comb their hair daily with the appropriate type of stainless steel comb. Bathe your Persian at least once a week, to keep them smelling their best, and make the most of their beautiful coat.

Intelligence

Persians are deceptive in quite a few ways, as they look so good. However, behind those captivating eyes is a brain which needs stimulating, so don't neglect it. They thrive on people's company, but also love to solve puzzles, so buy some appropriate puzzle toys as recommended by your vet. They are not demanding cats, so it's up to you to remember their mental requirements. If you're going to be away for hours on end, leave them some puzzles to solve with rewards at the end. Easier still, make sure your Persian always has the benefit of intelligent human company.

Other pet friendly

The Persian is fine with both people and animals, as long as you are considerate in the way you introduce them to your home. Remember, your home is also home to your Persian; they really should be put first before you allow strangers in. The Persian doesn't feel threatened by anything, so won't cause a fuss with other cats or dogs. If you already have pets, you need to introduce your Persian kitten as soon as possible, well before they are 6 months old. They will accept being down the pecking order, but only if they grow up knowing this.

Playfulness

The Persian likes to play, but not play rough. They are rewarding, and feel rewarded themselves, when the games involve cleverness; like finding things which have been hidden, or working out what goes where. In this way, they are perfect companions for young children, as they will help with a child's development. They don't mind boisterous company, but don't expect them to put up with being used as a punchbag; Persians are strong, capable cats and will get out of the way of aggressive people or pets very quickly. They always know what's going on, so they will find you before you know they're in the room.

4.5 out of 5

22

Siberian

The Siberian is a medium long haired cat whose coat is luxuriant and mainly white, with darker touches of various colours and in various places; but especially around its beautiful eyes and pointed ears. It has a double coat, part of which forms a magnificent ruff around its neck, giving it a look of an imperial Tsar from its home country. Siberians have round heads and stout bodies, which are helpful to preserve heat, and also make this a sturdy cat, weighing in at between 15 and 20 pounds; it's not unusual for a big male to tip the scales at 25 pounds.

Short history

As the name suggests, this magnificent cat hails from the Siberian region of Russia; one of the most cold and forbidding environments in the world. It is the national cat of Russia, which was shown off in high society during the late 19th Century, but remained a bit of a myth afterwards. It has only made an appearance in the USA since the fall of the Berlin Wall. As soon as it did so, however, it made an immediate impact, comparing favourably to established American and North European cats. As it is such a recently arrived breed, it is recognized by the International Cat Fanciers Association, under the title "Miscellaneous".

Personality

The Siberian has an explorer's personality, and will make mind boggling leaps into thin air; it's that kind of cat. They are endlessly curious, and will be sure to find ways to open or close things, creep into places and jump from one great height to another. The Siberian is a friendly cat, who values the company of both people and animals. Unlike other breeds, these are not demanding cats, so won't insist on being the centre of attention. Expect your Siberian to say hello when you come home, and follow you around while they figure out what you're up to.

Health

The Siberian is generally a very tough, healthy cat, as you'd expect from a creature from that part of the world. Like many other breeds of cat, however, they are susceptible to hypertrophic cardiomyopathy (HCM), a condition in the heart, where the muscle thickens up, making the organ less effective, and leading to a number of other conditions. You should be able to buy or adopt a Siberian kitten whose parents have been screened for this disease and found free of it, which reduces the chances of your own cat falling prey to the disease. Other than that, don't let your Siberian become obese, and you'll be fine.

Care

In terms of taking care of your Siberian, this will mainly consist of grooming and sticking to a healthy feeding regime. They are tough creatures who can look after themselves, but will always benefit from being properly cared for. Look after their coats, nails, eyes and ears, and give them some room to play about in. They are energetic cats, and will find ways to play, jump, climb and generally keep themselves active. Obesity is something you should guard against, and the Siberian is such a fine cat that you and your family will be tempted to please it with treats.

Grooming

The Siberian has a triple coat, which means it needs careful grooming. Their coats also change throughout the year, due to their inherited need to keep warm as the seasons change. They have extra hair on their rear legs, called britches, and their ruff (beard) grows especially thick during the autumn (fall), in preparation for winter. Despite all that, you only need to groom your Siberian once a week, as their fur does not get matted or knotted. This will change when spring approaches, as your cat will start to moult to get rid of its excess winter coat; this requires daily grooming.

Children and families

Siberians love kids, and kids in turn love them right back. They like to have human attention, and thrive when children show them as much. Kids also adore stroking their thick coats, and the Siberian loves to be stroked. One thing to remember about Siberians, however, is that they take longer than other cats to develop fully; in fact, a Siberian will not reach mature until it is 5 years old. Depending on the age of your children, you might have to remind them that the cat they've known for quite a while now is actually still a kitten.

Family friendliness

The Siberian will firmly establish itself at the heart of your family. This is partly because the whole family will adore it, want to stroke it, play with it and talk to it. The Siberian is well aware of its own charms, and will expect to be adored. This doesn't mean it's a diva, or expects to boss anyone around. They have such an even temperament that you'll probably find that any tensions within the family will disappear once everybody's beloved Siberian makes an appearance. From toddlers to great aunts or uncles, your Siberian will bring everyone together.

General health

All pedigreed cats will have some sort of health problem and any breeder who claims that their breed has no health or genetic problems is most likely not being truthful. As mentioned previously the Siberian is susceptible to hypertrophic cardiomyopathy a hereditary health issue that can be of concern. However, the Siberian is a medium-size to large cat who is strong and robust. A special feature about the Siberian is it matures slowly, and can take up to five years to reach full physical development.

Ease of grooming

Although the Siberian is a triple coated cat, the breed is easy to groom. Their dense hair requires the attention of a steel comb, to get rid of things your cat hasn't managed to remove itself. Grooming their coat once a week will ensure even distribution of oils along the length of each hair, and ensure a stunningly superb coat. Siberians enjoy being groomed, and will welcome the attention of any family member who wants to help them out. After that, it's just a question of getting them used to having their nails trimmed and teeth cleaned; until spring comes, when you'll have to up your game to a daily grooming routine.

Siberians have a high level of intelligence, which you should take into account before you buy or adopt one. They thrive on attention, especially when it involves games where they can get involved and help solve puzzles with the family. The Siberian is also emotionally intelligent, and will use this intelligence to help people get along, with themselves included at every stage, of course. They are not demanding like some other cats, so you won't hear them complaining about being bored or ignored; however, these are things you should avoid, and try to keep your Siberian engaged as much of the time as possible.

Other pet friendly

If you have other pets, or if you're expecting guests who have, you shouldn't have too many problems with your Siberian. They like the company of other cats, which don't necessarily have to be Siberians themselves. They'll also get along fine with dogs, as long as they are well enough behaved. Socialization is always essential when introducing cats to other animals, so take advice from your vet about this. As the Siberian is an extremely sociable cat, it will want the same thing as you do; a peaceful home where people and pets have fun together.

One thing the Siberian is especially noted for is its love of feathers. It is instantly fascinated by feathers, and its attention will be rapt as soon as it sees a feathered toy. It'll try and catch it with one paw, and follow every little movement with great intensity. There are feathered toys available especially designed to keep Siberians occupied; combine these with problem solving and you'll have one very happy cat. Your children will also love playing with your Siberian, so teach them how to use feathered toys properly and everybody's laughing, while being fascinated at the same time.

4.5 out of 5

Final Thoughts

Cat ownership is one of the most consistently high statistics in many Western countries. In the UK, supposedly a nation of dog lovers, more households (25%) actually own cats than dogs. In the US, that figure is nearly half, at a quite staggering 47%. The fact is that owning at least one cat makes a lot of people very happy. As they are independent, intelligent creatures, many people prefer cats because they are "lower maintenance" than dogs; and in some ways they are. For those who lead busy lives, not having to worry about getting home to exercise their pet can be relaxing in itself.

That should not mean, however, that you neglect your cat or cats if you choose to become a cat owner. As we hope we have shown throughout this guide, cats thrive on human company, from people of all ages, starting with babies all the way to the very elderly. If you live on your own, a cat can be the source of great comfort; if you have a family of any size, adding one or more feline members can be a huge asset to family cohesion, happiness and development.

Take your time to choose the right cat for your situation. Peruse this book at your leisure, and imagine one or more of these great breeds in your home. As you can see, there are many personality types to choose from; showman, lounger, lap cat, tough guy, softie, and a mixture of all of the above. From ancient breeds coming out of Asia to much more recent crosses, a cat's personality shines through in both its coat and its temperament.

Some people choose cats to show. For this purpose, there are longhairs, shorthairs, single coats and undercoats, in ranges of colours and patterns to make your head spin. Whether you show your cat or not, basic care is pretty much the same; once you agree a grooming, feeding and health check schedule with your vet, you'll be amazed at how easy it is to keep a cat happy and in good health.

Domestic cats can live up to 20 years. If you socialize them properly at a very young age, neuter them before 6 months and take care of their physical and mental health, you could have a clever, funny and genuinely warm companion for a long time. We hope our guide helps to make the right choice; enjoy your cat or cats, and spread the word on the world's best pets.